Power and Politics in Africa

A Boundary Generator

Takuo Iwata

Ritsumeikan University, Kyoto, Japan

Series in Politics

VERNON PRESS

www.vernonpress.com

In the Americas:	*In the rest of the world:*
Vernon Press	Vernon Press
1000 N West Street, Suite 1200,	C/Sancti Espiritu 17,
Wilmington, Delaware 19801	Malaga, 29006
United States	Spain

Series in Politics

Library of Congress Control Number: 2024938930

ISBN: 979-8-8819-0117-2
Also available: 979-8-8819-0038-0 [Hardback]; 979-8-8819-0086-1 [PDF, E-Book]

Cover design by Vernon Press.

Cover image: Le regard d'un continent © 2023 Oswald Adande.

Table of Contents

Acknowledgments

This book is the product of the research on power in African politics that I have been conducting since I was a Ph.D. candidate. For three decades, I have been reflecting on various power-related issues in African politics while conducting field research in African countries and elsewhere, participating in international and domestic conferences, and teaching my classes at graduate and undergraduate schools.

I express my gratitude to Langaa Publisher (Bamenda, Cameroon) for giving me permission to reproduce (with some modifications) my chapter "Political Satire and Laughter in Africa" in Ofusu-Kusi, Y., & Matsuda, M. (Eds.). (2020). *The Challenge of African Potentials — Conviviality, Informality and Futurity —*. I thank Centro de Investigaciones de Política Internacional (The International Policy Research Center, CIPI, Havana, Cuba) for the reproduction (with additional description) of my paper "Las relaciones entre Asia y Africa en el pasado y el futuro" in their journal *Cuadernos de Nuestra America* (No.6, 2022). I also acknowledge the International Studies Association of Ritsumeikan University (Kyoto, Japan) for allowing the reproduction (with some modifications) of my papers published in Volumes 15, 16, 17, 20, and 21 (in 2016, 2017, 2018, 2021, and 2022, respectively) of the journal *Ritsumeikan Annual Review of International Studies*.

I deeply appreciate the anonymous reviewers for their precious time and very insightful comments to improve the quality of this book. I sincerely thank Vernon Press, Mr. Batana, the director; Mr. Legatos and the editorial team; and the marketing and design team for all their efficient and kindest support in publishing this monograph book. However, any errors or misunderstandings are owing to the author. I also thank all collaborators, colleagues, and students in/from African, Asian, and Western countries for providing me with meaningful opportunities for learning and discussing. Last but not least, I want to express my gratitude to Kaya and Hanako, who have encouraged my work, sometimes with constructive criticism, in our house.

Kyoto, July 31, 2024

Takuo Iwata

Author's Biography

Takuo Iwata, Ph.D. (political science), Professor, Ritsumeikan University (Japan), teaches politics and international relations in Africa and Asia–Africa relations. He has published books and articles, such as *New Asian Approaches to Africa* (edited by Iwata, T., Vernon Press, 2020).

List of Abbreviations

AAGC: Asia Africa Growth Corridor

ABC: *Agência Brasileira de Cooperação* (Brazilian Cooperation Agency)

AfCFTA: African Continental Free Trade Area

AIIB: Asian Infrastructure Investment Bank

AMBF: *Association des municipalités du Burkina Faso* (Association of Municipalities of Burkina Faso)

AMM: *Association des municipalités du Mali* (Association of Municipalities of Mali)

ANCB: *Association nationale des communes du Bénin* (National Association of Communes of Benin)

AOF: *Afrique occidentale française* (French West Africa)

ASEAN: Association of Southeast Asian Nations

AU: African Union

BRI: Belt and Road Initiative

CDP: *Congrès pour la démocratie et le progrès* (Congress for Democracy and Progress)

CIDCA: China International Development Cooperation Agency

DPA: Development Partnership Administration

ECOWAS: Economic Community of West African States

FCBE: *Forces cauris pour un Bénin émergent* (Cowrie Forces for an Emerging Benin)

FOCAC: Forum of China–Africa Cooperation

FOIP: Free and Open Indo-Pacific

GDP: Gross Domestic Product

IAF: Indonesia–Africa Forum

IAFS: India–Africa Forum Summit

ICJ: International Court of Justice

ITEC: Indian Technical and Economic Cooperation

JETRO: Japan External Trade Organization

JICA: Japan International Cooperation Agency

KOAF: Korea–Africa Forum

MPP: *Mouvement pour le peuple et progrès* (Movement for People and Progress)

NAM: Non-Aligned Movement

NIEO: New International Economic Order

OAU: Organisation of African Unity

OECD–DAC: Organisation for Economic Co-operation and Development – Development Assistance Committee

PPB: (*le*) *Politique par le bas* (Political thing from below)

SSC: South–South Cooperation

SSTrC: South–South Triangular Cooperation

TICAD: Tokyo International Conference on African Development

UN: United Nations

UNSC: United Nations Security Council

WABI: West African Borders and Integration

List of Tables

List of Figures

Political Map of Africa

Source: Nations Online Project

Introduction

This book aims to reflect on power in African politics and international relations by revisiting its origin, definition, mechanisms, and functions through theoretical (conceptual) reflections and case studies.

It is always significant to study power in African politics. Power has been the engine of politics. It is also the goal of players of political games. Power is invariably the central question in decoding political issues. More critically, power affects people's behaviors, especially those of political actors, and leads to crucial consequences. It is a prominent character of power in African politics.

What is (political) power? Power has been an essential concept in political science worldwide for at least 2,000 years. Although studies in political science have reflected on power, we have not necessarily reached a definitive conclusion on how to define the concept of power. Unanswered questions remain in political science: What is power, and how does it influence our behavior? Despite being an essential engine or mechanism in politics, power remains a subject to be tackled in political science. The concept of power is a classical but constantly renewed subject and goal in the thousands of years of political study.

In reflecting on the concept of power in African politics, this book highlights that power is an essential boundary generator that creates gaps in people's everyday lives, society, the political arena, and international relations. The book, therefore, examines power to understand African politics. Power creates, maintains, and changes the gaps and differences in all arenas of human life. Boundary-generating power fosters political dynamism, which accompanies asymmetrical political relations.

In the twenty-first century, the political situation in African countries has progressively changed, as have the economic and social circumstances. The images of politics and international relations in Africa should be re-examined as the contemporary world's political environment has changed in the globalizing post-Cold War era.

Three decades have passed since the dawn of democratization on the African continent in the early 1990s. Some African countries have attempted democratization and reshaped their political structure, and political freedom has consequently spread in these countries. Other countries, unfortunately, have experienced the revival of authoritarian regimes or serious armed conflicts in the post-Cold War era. Democratization has significantly influenced power management in African politics. This book aims to reflect on how democratization has impacted the behaviors of political actors and citizens. The book also examines how democratization has (re-)drawn boundaries between political regimes in African countries.

Several years after the dawn of democratization, African countries began initiating decentralization reforms. Initially, decentralization was considered an administrative reform to achieve administrative efficiency by devolving financial, technical, and human resources from the central government to local governments. However, decentralization was not a simple administrative reform. It reactivated political dynamism in local communities, resulting in the redrawing of boundaries between national and local politics. Decentralization stimulated political engineering among local political actors and encouraged international cooperation among local governments.

Since gaining independence from European colonies (with some exceptions), almost all African countries have faced sovereign border issues and disputes with neighboring countries. The sovereign border has been both an old and new challenge among African countries. Most current African borders were drawn during the colonial period and inherited as sovereign borders on the day of independence. Besides conflicts and disputes, these African borders have caused inconvenience, illegal trade, and the separation of historically and culturally established communities. Many border problems between neighboring African countries remain ongoing. Borders have created, impacted, maintained, and renewed boundaries among African states, especially among borderland people.

Many challenging situations have arisen due to borders in Africa's postcolonial history. Yet African borders also provide potential opportunities to bridge neighboring countries, strengthen inter-state security, and build regional integration. Cross-border local cooperation is a potential transborder cooperation measure. The current borderlands were not necessarily border regions in the precolonial time but were trade, immigration, and cultural meeting and exchange points. Therefore, the current borderland people and communities have long shared common cultural, economic, and linguistic practices. Supposedly, decentralization accelerates cross-border local cooperation in Africa. We must also recognize the positive and potential aspects of generating boundaries.

International circumstances also affect African politics and societies. Once the United States' unipolar hegemony began fading at the beginning of the twenty-first century, (re-)emerging global powers, such as Brazil, China, India, Indonesia, Russia, and Turkey, expanded their influence in Africa by enthusiastically appealing for a multipolar international order. As the world's geopolitical order has changed, transforming geopolitical power relations affects politics and international relations in African countries. International circumstances have changed dramatically for developing countries in the transition from the solidarity of the Third World during the Cold War time to the emergence of the Global South in the era of globalization. The inter-continental relations between Asia and Africa are not exceptional but typical. Since the Asian–African conference (Bandung, 1955), Asia–Africa relations have been described in terms of solidarity and neutrality, within the Cold War context, as equal partners through South–South cooperation. However, as some Asian countries have achieved significant economic development and emerged as worldwide economic giants, the economic gap between the two continents has expanded significantly and become more apparent. The relationship between Asia and Africa has transformed from one of equal partners striving for Third World solidarity to one of asymmetrical partners in development assistance provision and reception through a more business-friendly South–South cooperation framework. Thus, South–South cooperation exposes the new boundaries in the Global South in the twenty-first century.

Since the end of the Cold War in the early 1990s, we have continuously observed political changes in Africa, from state politics to people's everyday acts. As the circumstances of politics and international relations in Africa have changed, political actors and ordinary people's political and social behaviors have transformed. However, we have also observed enduring challenges in African politics. For example, state- and nation-building, the rule of law, freedom of expression, transparency, and human rights remain challenging issues in African politics.

Political power or engineering affects the lives of not only political actors but also powerless ordinary people, who often suffer from absurd consequences caused by power-struggling political actors. Ordinary citizens usually cannot directly protest a powerful authoritarian regime. However, they do have some modest weapons they can wield against the regime and its leader. For instance, instead of direct protest, ordinary people caricature by mocking and laughing off their leader indirectly and metaphorically. Laughter is an essential act for human beings at all times. Although laughter does not change the political situation on its own, it might undermine the symbolic power of the political authority and its leader and ephemerally invert the feeling of the power relations between the ruling and ruled actors. Although laughter has not been a traditional research subject in political studies, it should not be neglected when reflecting on the symbolic boundaries between the ruling and ruled actors by focusing on the behavior of powerless ordinary citizens.

As political challenges unavoidably relate to the practices of (political) power, we must acknowledge that power is always essential to understanding Africa's politics and societies. Power is not only the political engine (means) but also a goal for political actors and their supporters. Historically, power has created, maintained, and changed boundaries in and among African states and societies physically, symbolically, and spiritually. This book emphasizes that power is a (politically) human-made boundary generator in African politics and societies. This book aims to tackle how power relates to these political challenges.

A politically made boundary creates gaps that manifest, maintain, undermine, and change power relations while influencing people's lives. Political and social boundaries have accompanied many dramas in Africa. Boundaries exist in political regimes, administrative units, sovereign borders, cross-border engagements, inter-continental relations, the Global South, symbolic political acts, colonial legacy (language), and the performers in the entertainment industry, which this book addresses. Boundaries are generated and work individually and in intertwining contexts.

First, this book addresses the conceptualization of power and then examines issues concerning power in African politics. The following chapters examine various power-related subjects, including democratization, decentralization, border issues, cross-border cooperation, Asia–Africa relations, and laughter in politics. The aim is to clarify the meaning, mechanisms, and functions of power in African politics and societies after about half a century of independence. The following chapters structure this book.

Chapter 1 reflects on the concept of power as a boundary generator in African politics. The political situation has changed throughout Africa in the twenty-first century as the world has become increasingly globalized. Three decades after the end of the Cold War and the initiation of democratization in African countries, reviewing and modifying the perceptions of African politics and international relations has become more necessary. Although we have observed significant changes in African politics, some challenges remain. Issues such as state-building, democratization, the rule of law, and human rights continue to be crucial political challenges for the future of Africa. These challenges in African politics unavoidably raise questions about the concept of (political) power in terms of its definition, meaning, and function. Therefore, we recognize that power is always the core component of understanding politics in Africa, despite changes in its character according to the time and political stage. Power is not only a political engine but also the goal of political activities. The concept of power in contemporary African politics has been thoroughly discussed but is always undergoing renewal. This chapter revisits the concept of power from the general context of political science to focus on political issues in Africa. Then, it reflects on the meaning and function of power as a boundary generator in contemporary African politics.

Chapter 2 revisits democratization, which has accompanied hope and disillusionment in African countries since the 1990s. African countries and people have experienced dramatic political transformation and turbulence from authoritarian regimes led by military leaders or the replacement of a one-party system to a multi-party system to promote political freedom and participation. However, conflicts and civil wars have also occurred in some African countries. Thus, democratization is still one of the most crucial political milestones in Africa's postcolonial political history and remains the most serious challenge in contemporary African politics. Democratization makes the boundaries between African countries clearer in terms of political development. First, this chapter briefly traces Africa's postcolonial political history. Second, this chapter examines the political impacts, problems, and challenges of democratization in contemporary African countries by focusing on the factors and actors that have been involved in democratization. Third, this chapter reflects on how democratization in Africa has been examined and understood both positively and negatively. Finally, this chapter presents a more comprehensive image of democratization to understand one of the most epoch-making political events in postcolonial African history.

Chapter 3 examines the political impact of decentralization in African countries. Decentralization is an outstanding phenomenon among the ongoing administrative and political reforms undertaken in recent decades around the world, and it has had significant political effects in African countries. In addition, urbanization amplifies the political impact of decentralization. Decentralization and urbanization have expanded the economic and political gaps between local governments in urban and rural areas as devolution has progressed from central to local governments. Decentralization encourages international cooperation between local governments and (non-)African partners. Decentralization and international cooperation between local governments have significantly influenced local politics in Africa. The decentralization process has changed the relationship between the state and local governments and between the local governments and residents, and it has drawn various boundaries in Africa's domestic politics and international relations. First, this chapter briefly traces the history of decentralization in Africa. Second, it reflects on the impact of decentralization on African politics and international relations by focusing on local elections, decentralized cooperation, and political disputes in urbanizing local governments in Benin and Burkina Faso. This is an appropriate time to examine local governments closely to understand Africa's political and social transformations through decentralization.

Chapter 4 reviews the border-related history and challenges in African countries by examining the case of Burkina Faso (former Upper Volta), which has endured complicated border disputes with neighboring countries since its independence. On the one hand, borderland regions in African countries have attracted worldwide attention in recent years as locations for activities by jihadist groups. On the other hand, borders are recognized as providing opportunities to advance economic and political cooperation and regional integration in the twenty-first century. The African Union expects the borders to transform "from barriers to bridges" among African countries and promote international cooperation in the borderlands. At independence, most African countries inherited colonial borders that had been demarcated by European empires since the late nineteenth century. Even almost half a century after the independence of African countries, the border-originated issues of African countries continue to cause conflict in political, economic, social, and international relations, which are closely connected with security concerns, such as conflict, ethnic division, refugees, or smuggling. The geographical and administrative boundaries keep affecting African countries' politics, economics, and international relations. This chapter examines the origin of border issues in Burkina Faso (Upper Volta) by referring to archival documents of the French colonial government. The chapter seeks to clarify the historical challenges and potential of African borders.

Chapter 5 reflects on regional security issues in West Africa, especially in Burkina Faso, focusing on international cooperation among local governments and border issues. When considering the recent political history of West African countries, domestic political disputes or conflicts are likely to become international and regional issues across national borders. Conflicts that occurred in Côte d'Ivoire and Mali in the twenty-first century directly affected the security and economic situations in neighboring countries. In Burkina Faso, which was facing a huge popular insurgency, President Compaoré unexpectedly stepped down after 27 years of his authoritarian regime. In addition to the destabilization of northern Mali, this unforeseen political turnover alarmed the international community about regional security in West Africa. The borders between sovereign states may not necessarily be barriers for extremist groups but occasionally convenient and permeable shields. By contrast, these borders remain strict and impermeable walls for the national armies of African states. First, this chapter addresses border issues in Burkina Faso. Border problems immediately translate to serious economic difficulties and security concerns for Burkina Faso as a landlocked country. Second, this chapter aims to decode security issues in West Africa while considering case studies in Burkina Faso and its neighboring countries to examine questions about borders and local governments' cooperation with neighboring countries.

Chapter 6 reflects on Asia–Africa relations by tracing the history since independence and the Non-Aligned Movement and overviewing the current transformation of intercontinental relations. Asian and African regions dramatically expanded and changed their economic and diplomatic relations in the twenty-first century, while the Global South became more influential in the new world economic and political order. Four major Asian countries—China, India, Japan, and South Korea—became more visible and influential in Africa. Other emerging Southeast Asian countries have subsequently followed this trend. These Asian countries have regularly hosted Africa forums for development and investment in the twenty-first century. The economic and political situation has become more diversified, accompanying significant gaps between Asian and African countries and regions. Consequently, the boundaries between Asia and Africa regarding economic development and international presence have become more visible. Asian partners have strived to implement new approaches to Africa. In the new world order, the structure of international cooperation began to transform. We observe more South–South and South–North triangular cooperation in Africa to decode the contemporary transformation of Asia–Africa relations over the years. Transforming Asia–Africa relations has accelerated a new trend in international cooperation. Unequal economic development creates a different gap and boundary between Asia and Africa by causing the emergence of a new type of donor–recipient relations.

Chapter 7 addresses laughter as a political communication intermediary in African countries by examining the meaning and potential of laughter and political satire in African politics. Political satire mirrors the political realities, trends, and changes and is often accompanied by laughter. Laughter is a symbolic weapon for both sides—the ruler and the ruled. On the one hand, powerful rulers use laughter to kill their opponents symbolically. On the other hand, otherwise powerless actors (or ordinary people) can also use laughter in a more satirical way. Although laughter does not directly change the political reality, we cannot neglect its meanings and influences in political communication. Political satire occasionally triggers an ephemeral and symbolic inversion of power in the relationship between powerful rulers and powerless people. Laughter-related acts practiced by ordinary and (politically) powerless people can undermine the symbolic power of the political authority and temporarily invert a political boundary between the ruling and ruled actors. It might induce real political change in the future. Laughter (or humor) would bring about a different way of thinking about political power among people.

Chapter 1

Reflection on the Concept of Power as a Boundary Generator in African Politics[1]

The study of politics is concerned with power. (Chabal 2009, 16)[2]

1.1. Introduction

We have observed numerous political dramas in Africa's postcolonial history, such as the Congo Crisis, the Biafran War, one-party regimes, Ujamaa socialism, a series of coups d'état, Cold War circumstances, Marxist-Leninist revolutions, democratization, post-Cold War conflicts, Rwanda's genocide, the end of the apartheid regime, the independence of Eritrea and South Sudan, the jihadist movement, and so on. These dramas have been the consequences of struggles for the sake of state power and other political goals.

This chapter aims to enrich the understanding of politics and politically influenced life in Africa while rethinking the concept of (political) power. In studying African politics, must we still tackle this rather exhausted concept? Power is omnipresent in all scenes of human activity and is considered the catalyst, engine, or goal of a political struggle, even if it is neither visible nor measurable in a comprehensive way. Although power is indispensable for running all political processes, this concept remains ambiguous in terms of its definition, function, mechanism, structure, theory, and analytical tool in the study of politics. Indeed, power has been the first and ultimate question throughout the long history of political science.

---

[1] This chapter was originally published in the journal of the International Studies Association of Ritsumeikan University (Kyoto, Japan): Iwata, T. (2017). Rethinking the concept of power in African politics — A boundary producer —. *Ritsumeikan Annual Review of International Studies, 16*, 19–36. The author thanks the International Studies Association of Ritsumeikan University for the permission to reprint this article.

[2] Chabal (2009, 40) argues, "Political science is concerned with the exercise of power, which all too often is unthinkingly assimilated to authority. However, the two are different in ways that matter. Power can be approached from a variety of different angles but it essentially entails the ability to force others to comply; by coercion if necessary. Authority implies a position of trust, competence and wisdom that confers upon those who are endowed with it the force of persuasion, rather than coercion."

> Power is one of the most central and at the same time most contentious concepts in the social sciences. The debates on what is 'power', and how it can be defined and conceptualized, rank among the most enduring themes of all academic disciplines that deal with power — political science, political sociology, political philosophy, political anthropology, and so forth. Yet, there is no satisfactory outcome as to what power actually means. (Harakova 2011, 9)

Before tackling this conundrum, we also need to reflect on what politics is. This concept itself remains controversial in the field of political science. It is too immense an objective for this modest book to seek a comprehensive definition of politics. However, in this book, politics is principally defined as human and institutional activities in which each motivated actor (individual, group, community, state, etc.) makes, maintains, and transforms symmetrical or asymmetrical relations through mutual actions with a particular goal and strategy.

Power is always the engine of political activities aimed at changing or maintaining the political order and balance. The field of political activities exists not only in the political society—which is composed of individuals, groups, and communities—for the professional pursuit of political goals but also in the civil society—which is composed of associations not necessarily founded for political achievements but occasionally for involvement in political issues. Power encompasses not only the means of achieving objectives and implementing ideas but also the goals of political activities. In fact, we cannot pursue any political activity without grasping this invisible but certainly influential force. This book constitutes an attempt to reflect on how political actors and people in Africa have struggled for power and remained in power or escaped from it.

Africa's postcolonial political history has been described primarily in terms of political instability. Just after African countries gained independence, rivalries and conflicts occurred among political, military, and ethno-regional groups to establish political regimes, build nation-states, and emerge victorious in elections or disrupt order. Contemporary African history is marked by millions of victims and refugees from political violence, such as military coups d'état and civil wars. In those early days of independence, political instability, rather than political liberty or democracy, was the most serious concern for newly established African states. Therefore, African leaders adopted a more authoritarian political system, such as a one-party system or military regime. During the Cold War, Western countries, with their own interests, practically allowed and even supported such authoritarian African regimes. Indeed, the struggle for state power is a feature of postcolonial African politics. Throughout contemporary

African political history, the concept of power has remained the core issue for understanding African politics.

Throughout the history of political science, scholars and thinkers have repeatedly questioned and pondered the concept and theories of power. The concept of power has long been dissected; nevertheless, it always requires a renewed and different understanding depending on the situation and era. This chapter aims to advance the understanding of the concept of power in reflections between the general context elaborated in Western-based political thought and the realpolitik (or historicity) experienced on African soil. Thus, the chapter focuses on the concept of power from various perspectives to understand political dynamism in Africa.

1.2. Conceptualization of Power

Political power is much more specific. Politics is all about power: about how political agents create, compete for, and use power to attain public goals that, at least on the surface, are presumed to be for the common good of a political community. Yet just as often and more covertly, political power is used to attain private goals for the good of agents involved. Without power, political agents, especially political leaders, are ineffective and probably ephemeral. (Kurtz 2001, 21)

We have yet to achieve consensus on any unique or final definition of power in political science. The confusion of interpreting power is owing to the fact that there are various ways of understanding this concept. Although this chapter does not pursue the theoretical challenge of seeking the ultimate definition of power, we cannot examine how power works in African politics without a conceptualization of power. This chapter first addresses the concept of power in comparison to exponent understandings. Then, it demonstrates this book's understanding of this concept and point of view as an analytical framework for studies on African politics.

One of the most common and dominant understandings of the concept of power is recognized as the Weberian manner in social science. Many political scientists have been influenced by Max Weber or started thinking from/with Weber's idea. Weber (1971) defines power as the probability that an actor will be in a position to carry out his own goals in a social relationship despite resistance.

Lukes classifies pro-Weberian scholars who have discussed power. For Russell, power is "the production of intended effects." Dahl's intuitive and simplistic idea of power is that "A has power over B to the extent that he can get B to do something that B would not otherwise do." These understandings of power may be traced to Weber. However, these approaches have been criticized as "misconceived or too narrow" (Lukes 1986, 1–3) because they might neglect the uncertainty of measuring political actors' will (Sugita 2000, 13).

Lukes also classifies anti-Weberian views on the definition of power. For Persons, "Power is a system resource, a 'generalized facility or resource in the society,' analogous to money, which enables the achievement of collective goals through the agreement of members of a society to legitimize leadership positions whose incumbents further the goals of the system, if necessary by use of negative sanctions" (Lukes 1986, 3). Arend rejects the suggestion that the question about power is who rules whom. For Arend, "power is 'not the property of an individual'; It 'corresponds to the human ability not just to act but to act in concert'" (Lukes 1986, 3). For Poulantzas, "power identifies the ways in which that system (*the 'ensemble of the structures'*) affects 'the relations of the practices of the various classes in conflict'" (Lukes 1986, 4).

Power has long been perceived as coming from the top to the bottom or radiating from the center to the periphery (Sugita 2000, 23). However, in contrast, Foucault argues that power does not unilaterally come from the center to the periphery as something that certain individuals and groups possess but is derived from the relationships among actors and is omnipresent in the non-unitary human activity space that influences human behaviors (cited in Sugita 2000, 27, 31). In addition, Foucault argues through the concept of *assujettissement* (subjugation) that a subjective actor simultaneously becomes an objective actor (Sugita 2000, 11).[3] Moreover, De La Boétie (1983) considers power as the choice to obey voluntarily or unconsciously.

Lukes (1986) categorizes power-related theories into three dimensions.[4] The first dimension is related to the study of concrete behaviors, such as observable

---

[3] Harakova (2011, 12–13) mentions, "The shift from power as force, to power as everything, stems from three intellectual sources: from Antonio Gramsci's concept of hegemony, and from the conceptualizations of power by each of Pierre Bourdieu, and Michel Foucault. Gramsci's concept of hegemony aims to embrace any kind of domination, including economic, cultural, or Western hegemony.... As he (Foucault) put it: "Power is everywhere, not because it embraces everything, but because it comes from everywhere.... Bourdieu incorporated the role of power and conflict as part of political relations in a practice theory while placing politics at its centre.... Bourdieu's symbolic power is a 'top-down' model based on 'social taxonomies' which subaltern groups 'misrecognize' as legitimate by failing to recognize them as arbitrary construction serving dominant class interests."

[4] According to Lukes (1986, 9–10), "The one-dimensional view of power, interests are seen as equivalent to revealed preferences — revealed, that is, by political behavior in decision making; to exercise power is to prevail over the contrary preferences of others, with respect to 'key issues'.... On the two-dimensional view of power advanced by Peter Bachrach and Morton Baratz, one exercises power in the manner the one-dimensionalists

conflicts between organized interests over a specific political issue. Most social scientists and theorists dealing with the concept of power (e.g., Weber, Dahl) view "power as domination" (Harakova 2011, 10). The second dimension of power goes beyond the analysis of observable conflicts and highlights hidden forces in nondecision-making (Bachrach & Baratz 1962). Finally, the third dimension of power "focuses on the most effective and treacherous use of power to prevent conflicts from arising" (Harakova 2011, 10).

Lukes (1986, 17) argues that "every attempt at a single general answer to the question addressing both the outcomes and the locations of power has failed and seems likely to fail." According to Seiyama (2000, 12–18), power is exercised at three levels: the individual level, the idealistic level, and the institutional level. However, the most common understanding of power is the first one, which reduces the power to the relationship between two individuals (also communities or states) who obviously have and exhibit a distinctive will.

Generally, we suppose violence, authority, and interest are means of wielding power. As Nye (2004, 2) mentions, "Power always depends on the context in which the relationship exists." Power never exists in a static condition or environment. It can be assumed and lost. However, we find a common objective in thinking about power that influences the behavior of the individual and the group. The idea that power is born, maintained, and changed through exchanges in human, social, and international relations is also broadly shared.

The author tentatively conceptualizes power as follows:

> Power is a potentiality that influences the behavior of actors (individuals, groups, communities, states, etc.) in relations, and it is established, maintained, and changed through mutual actions inside/outside institutions under the (mis-)perception of its resources and motives.

Although this definition might not cover every aspect related to the concept of power, it focuses on relations among actors and actions in the location where the power is exercised.

---

favour, but also by controlling the agenda, mobilizing the bias of the system, determining which are 'key' issues, indeed which issues come up for decision, and excluding those which threaten the interests of the powerful. Here interests adversely affected are shown by politically expressed preferences *and* extra-political or covertly expressed grievances and demands that are, in various ways, denied entry into the decision-making process. The three-dimensional view incorporates power of the first two kinds, but also allows that power may operate to shape and modify desires and beliefs in a manner contrary to people's interests."

1.3. Historicity of Power in African Politics

This part reflects on how power has kept its meaning and has significantly influenced African politics. We need to think about power as being based on the historical realities of African politics, not only on an ideology-oriented theory or thought. In African politics, power is a question of historicity. According to Mamdani (1996), reflecting on historicity is unavoidable when considering power in Africa. Referring to Bayart, Mamdani (1996, 10) argues that the political structure should be examined in a de-dramatized way, based on its historicity, not on an analogy of historical events in the Western world. For instance, the concept of civil society was enthusiastically discussed in African studies in the 1990s with an ideological motive based on "anti-state romanticism" (Mamdani 1996, 13, 18–19, 186).

Power has created boundaries in societies and between people all over the world throughout political history. Africa is no exception. Political power has created boundaries in African societies in incomplete and unequal ways. These human-made boundaries have led to discrimination and segregation. However, such boundaries are often permeable and porous, not only in a geographical sense but also in a socio-political sense. Mamdani is a scholar who is strongly aware of the politically fabricated boundaries in African societies while retracing to the colonial administration for understanding political problems in postcolonial Africa.

Mamdani presents the concept of "institutional segregation" to understand how power has been structured in African societies while reflecting on colonial governance. Institutional segregation was a core methodology for colonial authorities to establish and manage colonial "indirect" rule. Institutional segregation brought about boundaries in Africa that were not only about separating colonizers from colonized people, settlers from natives, citizens from subjects, urban from rural, and civilized from uncivilized, but also about fixing people in a defined ethnic or tribal unit as an "ahistorically" imagined social cliché (Mamdani 1996, 27, 51, 63, 79, 84, 91). This legacy of institutional segregation created "decentralized despotism" under colonial rule and was succeeded by postcolonial African countries transforming their character according to the time and political environment (Mamdani 1996, 18, 23).

Mamdani (1996, 61) argues that this system of decentralized despotism created an octopus-like structure of political power in the colonial system, where each colonial unit was autonomous, but not independent. This was accompanied by territorial segregation in the apartheid system of South Africa (Mamdani 1996, 5–6). According to Mamdani, this institutional segregation was not an exceptionally unique structure or invention of South Africa but was found in other colonial systems (Mamdani 1996, 7). The independence of

African countries de-racialized the state. However, the independence neither democratized African states necessarily nor indigenized civil society institutions (Mamdani 1996, 136, 289).

Colonial rule distinguished citizens from subjects, which also inflexibly categorized the local African people. African subjects were confined to and positioned in traditional tribal communities on the opposite side of citizenship (Mamdani 1996, 48–49, 91). Under indirect rule, tribes were actors of custom planting "indigenous" culture and authorities (Mamdani 1996, 51, 286). As a result, colonial rule brought about a "decentralized" dictatorship with institutional force. Under this style, chieftaincy was reformed and invented during colonial rule (Banégas 2003, 38), even if it was not a totally "colonial" fiction. Chiefs strengthened their power and status by monopolizing the legislative, judicial, administrative, and police functions under the colonial structure (Mamdani 1996, 53). Thus, the chief became the absolute leader of a rural area (Mamdani 1996, 54). This decentralized despotism exacerbated the urban–rural division as well as the divisions among ethnic groups (Mamdani 1996, 291). Independence destroyed the chief's political power, which had been allowed and maintained on the edge of the colonial system.

The political legacy of decentralized despotism bequeathed by colonial governance affected the character of the state in postcolonial African countries. African states might be inclined to pursue management that is informal and personalized. This chapter reflects on power in postcolonial African politics from the view of the human network as one that is neither necessarily center–periphery nor top–bottom in structure. The "publicness" of the state could not necessarily be presumed as an ensured condition or reality to reflect on the state in Africa. A principal feature is that the state in the African context is more a "private" (or patrimonial) institution than a public one. In African countries, the state has been not only the stage of political activities but also the goal in the struggle for power, to feed supporters and/or not to be devoured by opponents. There is still considerable room for "politics of the belly" (*la politique du ventre*, Bayart 2006) in the African state.

In the historicity of the state, the "public" space surrounded by sovereign borders, where "tradition," "custom," or "tribe" were found, fabricated, and manipulated by European colonizers and African leaders throughout the colonial period, has strongly affected state-building. The "reinvention of tradition" brought about the public space in the imaginary sphere (Banégas 2003, 311–12). It is likely thought, in general, that power has been concentrated in the hands of the head of state (President of the Republic) in African political history. The idea of "personal rule" (Jackson & Rosberg 1984) or "neopatrimonialism" (Médard 1990) has been frequently discussed for decades. We have assumed that a president's will is carried out from top to bottom. However, political power does not necessarily work in such a unique or unilateral direction.

Inspired by the work of Deleuze and Guattari, Bayart reflects on the idea of a "rhizome" to decode the human network intertwined with the power relationship in African countries. The power-producing structure is neither fixed nor necessarily executed from top to bottom nor from the center to the periphery. According to Bayart, the postcolonial state has existed in a rhizomatous human network comprising an infinitely variable multiplicity of networks whose underground branches join the scattered points of society rather than a typical root-modeled system. The conventional idea of this arboreal metaphor of the state is exhausted in theories (Bayart 2006, 272–73).

Bayart cites a Cameroonian proverb stating that "Goats graze where they are attached" (Bayart 2006, 288); thus, everyone cannot eat equally or in a unique way (Bayart 2006, 325). Moreover, this famous goat proverb ontologically reflects the idea of "I graze, therefore, I am" to describe the political realities in postcolonial Africa (*Cameroon Tribune* 1988, May 8–9, cited in Bayart 2006, 325). A Beninese citizen will trust a candidate who shows respect by saying frankly what is in his belly (Xomé), and the statement resonates with an imaginary power of invisible forces that are mainly felt in the belly (Banégas 2003, 472). Manducation (the act of eating or chewing) is always fundamental to the objectives and motives in African politics.

Although a few researchers have reflected on the concept of power to decode the structure and mechanism of African politics, Chabal straightforwardly challenges this most difficult and fundamental question. Chabal's insightful book *Power in Africa* (1992) is one of the most valuable works on power in African politics. Chabal (1992, 5) argues that the minimal definition of power is "the balance between control and consent which governs the relationship between ruler and ruled." He examines analytical concepts such as "political community," "political accountability," "state," "civil society," and "production" to understand political power in Africa.

According to Chabal (1992, 54, 56), political accountability determines political relations as an institutional, traditional, and symbolic mechanism and is more rooted than political legitimacy and a system of representation. Absolute power means a lack of power relation (Chabal 1992, 55–56), and power is based on the material product system (Chabal 1992, 5). Therefore, political power may not be produced by ideological thought.

Similar to Mamdani, Chabal (1992, 5) insists on the importance of history to understand contemporary African politics. Political analysis is not aimed at pursuing an ideology or ethic but at understanding the reality of politics. Although a norm is necessary, it should be distinguished from analytical works.

In terms of the legitimacy of power, Chabal mentions that there is little difference in whether leaders seize power through an election or a military coup (Chabal 1992, 212). The legitimacy of power is formed in the dialectic of the *realpolitik* between power and wealth (Chabal 1992, 216).

Hegemony and counter-hegemony are intertwined to seek a portion of resources brought by power (Chabal 1992, 228). An ethnic group is not necessarily a counter-hegemonic force against the national authority, as is usually assumed by Western scholars (Chabal 1992, 231). Since precolonial times, African societies have neither been unitary nor static but have maintained dynamic and complex relationships between individuals and communities (Chabal 1992, 40). Colonial rulers divided communities and geographic regions owing to misunderstanding and contingency (Chabal 1992, 41). Modernization had to be interpreted in the context of tradition. Tradition was not only sought by colonial authorities but also by nationalists struggling against colonial rule and asserting their own legitimacy (Chabal 1992, 46). Slogans uttered by nationalist leaders, such as Negritude, Consciencism, and African humanity, were reinterpretations of the past in order to establish the future nation-state (Chabal 1992, 47–48).

It is indispensable to review the system and structure of colonial rule to consider governance in contemporary Africa. In colonial regimes, the governor of the colony was the pseudo-king (Mamdani 1996, 74), whose governance relied on a balance of patronage and coercion (Chabal 1992, 172). It would be incorrect to interpret political development as a vector from "tradition" to "modernity" (Chabal 1992, 200). Colonial borders were permeable to allow massive movements of people to escape the heavy taxation and forced labor charged by the colonial authorities (Chabal 1992, 102). Labor and land became commodities in a colonial economy. The heavy taxation and forced labor under colonial rule destroyed the political system and moral economy in Africa (Chabal 1992, 105–06).

Chabal examines a genealogy of concepts related to power in Africa, such as "political development," "class," "underdevelopment," "revolution," and "democratization," as lost paradigms (Chabal 1992, 11–32). He points out that these theoretical frameworks are not based on the historicity of Africa. This remains an example of analogical thinking derived from Western experiences and history (Mamdani 1996, 8–9). Chabal also points out the problematic character of political development theory that lacks historical consideration of structural functionalism under a unilinear development idea. It neglects the significance of precolonial and colonial histories in postcolonial and contemporary Africa. This framework cannot grasp the context of ethnic problems, coups d'état, corruption, and dictatorship that have harassed African people (Chabal 1992, 11–15).

Based on Marxism, class theory emerged as a counter-argument to political development theory. However, Marxism and political development theory share the same problem regarding historicity. Class theory has been elaborated in the context of an "imaginary" class experienced in the Western world. In fact, historicity in Africa is more complicated than the ideal model of the Marxist class (Chabal 1992, 15–19). The (meaning of the) state is always the core issue in African politics. We can never understand African politics while neglecting the historical context of the soil (Chabal 1992, 68). Underdevelopment theory is also a theory-biased approach referring to Western history, but is hardly based on African historicity. It persists in understanding from the world-system theory and lack of attention to the features of African politics. Therefore, underdevelopment theory is insufficient for appropriately analyzing African politics (Chabal 1992, 19–23).

Revolution theory was used to support armed struggles for independence in Angola, Guinea Bissau, Mozambique, and Zimbabwe and influenced African socialism in connection with Marxism-Leninism. According to Chabal, however, the revolutionary theory failed to describe the process of independence and state-building due to the imaginary and confused understanding of a nationalist people's war and socialist revolution (Chabal 1992, 23–28).

1.4. Power in Contemporary African Politics

The mode and style of power-related practices have been neither unique nor static but various and dynamic as the conditions of domestic politics and international relations have changed. The end of the Cold War and the wave of democratization in the Third World had a huge political impact across Africa. After the dissolution of the Soviet Union, Western countries drastically changed their behavior toward African countries while straightforwardly requesting political and economic reform or liberalization as a condition for foreign aid— so-called conditionality. Owing to the heavy financial and technical dependence on foreign aid, many African governments had to agree to these conditions. In addition to such external pressures, internal movements for democratization that came from outside the dominant political force increased the support from the people and civil society. African countries faced the biggest momentum for political change after independence. The beginning of the 1990s became one of the most crucial turning points in postcolonial African political history.

Although we have observed immense political momentum throughout postcolonial African history, democratization might be one of the most outstanding political events in Africa in terms of both domestic and international political circumstances. Democratization was a crucial political crossroad for African countries. These countries reached very different points after democratization was initiated, from its gradual consolidation to a return to an authoritarian regime, political instability, or civil war in extreme cases. Democratization was not only launched after enthusiastic demands from the people and civil society but was also a strict requirement from the "international community"—in other words, major Western aid donor countries. After the end of the Cold War, African countries faced a dramatic change in the world order and needed to survive in the new environment of international relations. It was almost impossible for any African leader to continue rejecting the wave of demands, both domestically and internationally, for democratization.

How has democratization (or lack thereof) influenced and changed the political power in contemporary Africa? Democratization movements significantly destabilized the power structure of authoritarian regimes in African countries. Democratization was expected to be the "Second Liberation" of Africa at the beginning of the 1990s, replacing the previous authoritarian political structure with a more democratic political regime. However, we have observed that the route of democratization has been neither unique nor straightforward among African countries in the last three decades.

Democratization not only changed the political structure of power but also created new politically fabricated boundaries between African countries, societies, and people. Democratization can alter or redraw boundaries relating to political power within and outside of a country. When democratization is more consolidated, political actors face more pressure to turn to voters to grant them access to state power through elections. In more democratized countries, political actors require different talents to be (re-)elected compared to the past one-party regime. Although it remained essential to exhibit loyalty to the state leader, this was not enough to ensure and promote one's political status. It became incumbent on political actors to evince their own popularity and financial capacity to meet the requests of their supporters and constituents as democratization progressed.

In international relations, democratization drew a boundary relating to the reputation between more and less democratization-friendly countries or opposing countries in Africa. The practice of democratic governance has been reflected in foreign aid; this was especially so in the early 1990s. However, this trend of linking democratization to foreign aid disappeared gradually during the decade after African countries began democratization, especially in the twenty-first century, with the coming of emerging countries, such as China and India, on the stage of international cooperation in Africa as giant South–South Cooperation partners.

After the optimistic years of the dawn of democratization were over, the international community began to recognize the stagnation of democratization or the return to authoritarianism in politics in African countries. Democratization did not automatically bring about democratic governance as Western donor countries expected earlier. The international community, including United Nations organizations, launched a support program to push the democratization process in African countries. However, the logic of democratization assistance seemed to be biased in favor of the ideology of [linear] "political development" as a fiction of pluralism and the rule of law, not based on the political reality or historicity on the ground in African countries. The approach of the international organization-led democratization support program seemed too simplistic and naive.

In addition, support for democratization has tended to focus on elites in political society, neglecting social action from the bottom while over-evaluating the pressure from the international community and depending on a theory of procedural democracy (Banégas 2003, 480–81). In fact, most democratization process trials failed or resulted in strictly surface-level change, allowing the political structure of the "politics of the belly" (Banégas 2003, 479). Democratization changed the elites' faces but did not fundamentally change actors' political behaviors (Daloz 1999, 19). As Banégas mentions, we might observe this as "[changing] everything, not to change anything" (Banégas 2003, 303). However, democratization reshuffled the public (political) space and brought a certain political change of "governmentality" (*gouvernementalité*) between rulers and ruled people (Banégas 2003, 479).

Although democratization is a rather fragile process facing innumerable challenges, the institutionalization or regular repetition of elections (without any suspension by military coup d'état) unavoidably influenced and changed the behaviors and strategies of political actors. On the people's side, a competitive electoral system changed their minds that they were electing their leader, especially in the case of the President of a Republic. Democratization trembled and destabilized the former social order and morals of the state (Banégas 2003, 388). After the initiation of the democratization process, money became an influential factor in the political arena, especially during the electoral period. Money was able to buy people's minds (*achat des consciences*) more so in the electoral process than during the pre-democratization era (Banégas 2003, 440). This could be a universal phenomenon in the first years of a democratic transition.

Principally, we expect that democratization will change the behavior of the political elite. Political analysts were likely to consider politicians and military officers as the principal actors to be examined before democratization was launched. Through the democratization process, the concept of civil society has been focused on, and its involvement in nationwide decision-making has been encouraged. Thus, a new political and economic class was formed after political elites entered NGOs (Banégas 2003, 265–67).

The political struggle between the state and civil society generated a hegemony, which is a key issue in postcolonial African politics (Chabal 1992, 81). As the spotlight was focused on the concept of civil society and its actors, the possible boundary between the state and civil society became a question in African countries.

In contemporary African countries, civil society has been encouraged against the political totalization of the state (Chabal 1992, 135). However, the concept of civil society remains subjective, uncertain, unsustainable, and unreliable as an analytical framework in the academic domain. In addition, it remains a relative idea that can be defined in relation to the state (Chabal 1992, 85). Civil society in Africa is also the "combination of tradition and modernity" (Chabal 1992, 88).

Democratization-related theories are certainly meaningful for understanding African politics from a universal perspective. Democratization made a point of low politics or politics at the individual level. However, this approach exposes the insufficiency of reconsidering the "individual" in African political analysis. The concept of the individual is not necessarily similar to the Western idea. Some researchers departed from the reality of African historicity by over-considering the ideal typology of Western democracy (Chabal 1992, 28–32).

It is impossible to analyze African politics without understanding the political community (Chabal 1992, 53). Independence changed the relationship between the state and individuals (Chabal 1992, 79). In postcolonial Africa, the state preceded the construction of the nation (Chabal 1992, 47). The state in postcolonial Africa should be understood in terms of the relationship with other social institutions rather than according to a static structure or ideology. The rule of law is an important element for measuring the morality of political leaders (Chabal 1992, 165). This point has shown its importance in that some leaders have tried to modify the constitution to remove the article stipulating the limitation on the term of the presidency adopted after democratization started in the 1990s.

In the decentralization process undertaken for almost two decades, it seems that political resources gradually began to be deconcentrated. After decentralization started, local representatives (the Mayor and members of the local assembly) were directly elected by local residents. Local politics became a more focal issue through the devolution of power and finance from the central government to local governments. In contemporary Africa, we can no longer neglect local governance when examining democratization nor focus solely on the capital city. As Mamdani (1996, 289) mentions, democratization is inefficient without local governments' reform.

However, the beginning of the 1990s was not only known as a positive turning point in African politics but also as the coming of a decade of violence and conflicts, with some tragic cases, such as the genocide in Rwanda and the rule of warlords in Liberia and Sierra Leone, while political liberalization from apartheid and democratization were simultaneously occurring in South Africa.

Although conflict or civil war was not unique to postcolonial Africa, the character of such events changed in the 1990s, during the post-Cold War era. The stakeholders in such conflicts became more diverse. In post-Cold War conflicts, the boundary or distinction between perpetrators and victims became vaguer. Armed fights have not only been deployed between national armies and rebel forces but also among national/rebel forces mobilizing ordinary people, including children. Further, it was not only rebel forces but also national armies that were deliberately violating the rules of war and human rights and committing crimes during these conflicts. In the Rwandan genocide that occurred in 1994, ordinary people became perpetrators and killed neighbors with whom they had lived for decades. The conflicts in the 1990s in African countries exposed that the boundary between state power-holders and opponents had become increasingly blurred. Rebel groups were not necessarily seeking state power by occupying the capital city as the ultimate goal of their activities.

Conflict of this new character complicated social reconstruction and reconciliation after the end of an armed battle because ordinary people were broadly involved in the massacres, creating unerasable resentment in the minds of both victims and perpetrators. Many former rebel soldiers have been turned away from their own villages and even by their own families.

In the twenty-first century, the political situation in Africa has kept changing. In international relations, the traditional framework of North–South relations became less meaningful for comprehensively understanding international relations despite the renewed "Global South" label, especially after emerging countries expanded their influence across the African continent. In recent years, emerging countries, such as Brazil, China, India, and Indonesia, have strongly appealed for South–South cooperation. Western countries have faced the biggest challenge against the principle of foreign aid architecture — that is, that "rich," developed countries (practically OECD members) support "poor" developing countries. Developed countries can no longer survive without considering their relations with emerging countries. In the twenty-first century, the boundary between the aid donor and recipient persists despite the significant room for questioning or reconsidering while the world economic power balance has been fundamentally changing.

We must also point out that the sovereign borders between African states might be understood as porous and ambiguous ones. Since independence, African countries have been unable to exercise sufficient control over their borders due to their vast territories with scarce human and financial resources. In recent years, rebel forces have been able to cross borders relatively easier than before. Furthermore, the globalization of jihadists' activities has made the border-related situation increasingly complicated and delicate. The porous and vague borders between African states are favorable to jihadist groups, such as Al Qaeda or Islamic State, wishing to carry out and expand their operations. Rather than barriers, these borders are occasionally permeable and convenient shields behind which these groups can protect themselves. Although globalization did not remove the borders between states, it certainly changed the meaning and function of the border.

1.5. Conclusion

This chapter offered an introductory reflection on the concept of power in African politics. We must be careful of this concept to avoid over-generalizing its character, function, and meaning in African politics and conveying too simplistic an understanding because the cultural, economic, historical, religious, and social contexts are extremely diverse and complicatedly intertwined in each African country and society.

However, we have identified some common characteristics that structure the power in the political reality and historicity that African countries and people have experienced in their postcolonial history. A relatively common element on which this chapter has focused is that power fabricates and manipulates a boundary in the political arena as well as in communities and societies, and even among individuals, not only in the geographical sense but also in the cultural, economic, ethnic, religious, social, and especially political senses, as a result of repeated politically motivated acts. In addition, political power has brought about segregation among people, thereby separating the rulers from the ruled actors, citizens, and subjects, as Mamdani (1996) mentions in his idea of "institutional segregation." Power is a boundary generator in human society while accompanying political gaps and struggles.

Although this chapter proposed a tentative definition of power in the previous section, it complements an additional factor that could help develop a more comprehensive grasp of the concept of power. The author has tried to define the concept of power in politics as follows:

> [Political] Power is a potentiality that influences the behaviors of actors (individuals, groups, communities, states, etc.) in relations and that is established, maintained, and changed through mutual actions and

communications inside/outside institutions under the (mis-) perception of its resource and motive through incomplete information. Power enables one to draw, maintain, and transform boundaries between countries, societies, and people, often accompanied by inequality.

Although power draws a boundary between actors in the political arena, such a boundary is not an impermeable wall but a permeable and occasionally convenient membrane for actors working against/for/in/with power. This is a significant point when we think about power, which is used in everyday acts in African politics. In addition, African societies are highly "politicized" by/with boundaries. The idea of a "politics from below" (*le politique par le bas*), discussed by Bayart and his comrades, is keen to focus on this permeable and porous character of power derived from the boundary between how "ruled" actors undermine the "established" power seeping through the political and social boundaries.

As a tentative conclusion, it is still useful and unavoidable to examine the issues of African politics in light of the concept of power while remaining conscious of the boundaries in African societies.

Chapter 2

Revisiting Democratization in Contemporary African Politics: Boundaries between Political Regimes[1]

When the "third wave" of democratization hit the African continent, there was an outburst of optimistic scholarship voicing hopes for a "second liberation" that soon turned into sour commentaries on the lack of "real" change. (Lindberg 2009, 25)

2.1 Introduction

In February 1990, the national dialogue forum, *La conférence nationale des forces vives de la nation* (The National Conference of Active Forces of Nation, Iwata 2000; 2004), took place in Cotonou, Benin, to reassess the political history since independence and launch political reform toward democracy. The holed jar became a symbol of the National Conference and then the democratization of Benin.

The fingers of the people of Dahomey cover this jar's holes. In the nineteenth century, King Ghezo (Guézo, reigned 1818–58) called for the unity of the Dahomean people. This holed jar symbolized solidarity for the freedom of the Dahomey kingdom (Piqué & Rainer 1999, 30, 59). The holed jar was revived as the symbol of a pivotal moment of democratization in Benin to tackle the crucial political challenge with the people's solidarity.

Since the 1990s, Africa's political, economic, and social circumstances have significantly changed. Africa is no longer the hopeless continent (including archipelagic countries) where people live under miserable poverty, conflict, and a brutal dictatorship, even if these issues remain serious challenges. African countries are no longer destined to be viewed as incurable patients or untalented students by the international (aid) community (de facto Western donor countries). Meanwhile, some European countries suffered a severe economic crisis in the late 2000s, and economists and policymakers worldwide

---

[1] This chapter was originally published in the journal of the International Studies Association of Ritsumeikan University (Kyoto, Japan): Iwata, T. (2022a). Rethinking democratization in contemporary African politics. *Ritsumeikan Annual Review of International Studies, 21,* 1–27.

began to expect Africa to be the locomotive of world economic growth. Consequently, African voices became more influential and listened to worldwide over the subsequent years.

Figure 2.1. Statue of the Holed Jar

Source: Author (October 2005, Bohicon, Benin)

In the 2010s, African countries celebrated 50 years of independence. However, scholars of politics and journalists have been more likely to highlight bitter political experiences in postcolonial African history. Indeed, we have witnessed many tragic conflicts or long and brutal authoritarian regimes in African countries, especially before the dawn of democratization.

In recent years, democracy has been highlighted again as a focal issue in international relations. The US government hosted the Summit for Democracy at the end of 2021 and invited about 110 countries to attend, excluding China, Russia, and other potential adversaries (US Department of State 2021). Democracy again became the US alliance's ideological weapon in the New Cold War framework.

Since the 1990s, the post-Cold War time, political regimes in African countries have been diversified compared to the three previous decades (the 1960s–1980s), when Africa's political history had principally been described under the one-party regime and its toppling by a military coup d'état. Democratization trials accompanied the diversification of political regimes and situations in the 1990s on the African continent. Democratization is a political reform to bring about more political competition and participation. The wave of democratization provided the opportunity for the African people to be involved in the decision-making. Democratization accompanied freedom of expression and activated political debates. Some (not many, unfortunately) African countries have kept track of democratization even while experiencing some challenges. In other countries, political leaders resumed authoritarian rule after fake political reform, which enabled political manipulation despite maintaining multi-party elections. In the worst cases, the political confusion during the transition to democracy caused civil war. Nevertheless, the number of military coups d'état was reduced during the democratization transition in the 1990s.

In the 2020s, many African countries still suffer from political instability and violence, and many African people still live under multi-party (or electoral) authoritarian rule. However, people keep enjoying a politically freer life while consolidating constitutional democracy in some African countries. This contrasting situation draws a boundary between democratizing and authoritarian politics on the African continent. Three decades after the democratization trials began in African countries, a distinction (boundary) between consolidating democracies and stubborn (or returned) authoritarian regimes and between politically freer societies and restricted societies became visible. The democratization experiences have significantly impacted African people's lives.

This chapter aims to revisit the processes and experiences of democratization in African countries to examine its achievements, predicaments, and challenges and to review political perspectives on the coming era. Democratization is still one of the most crucial challenges and a political reform that has brought about the most significant political change in postcolonial African history. Although three decades have passed since democratization began on the African continent, it remains a crucial issue in African politics. In other words, the democratization experience covers approximately the second half of Africa's postcolonial political history. Therefore, this chapter roughly distinguishes two parts of Africa's postcolonial history: the pre-democratization and challenging democratization periods. The chapter revisits and examines the democratization process in African countries to understand the history and perspectives on African politics in the twenty-first century.

2.2. Overview of Democratization in Africa

2.2.1. Definition of the Concept of Democratization

Democratization is the process of transforming the political system into a more democratic one. However, the concept of democracy itself has not necessarily been understood in a unique way in political science, leaving the question "What is democracy?" open. In this chapter, the author understands democratization as the political reform process to ensure free political competition and broader political participation to establish a more liberal society principally by achieving the conditions described in the concept of polyarchy (Dahl 2000, 90–91).[2]

In studies on democratization in Africa, there has been a noticeable trend of analyses distinguishing two phases of the democratization process—namely, the democratic transition and democratic consolidation phases—to classify and understand this process. It seems relatively easier to study the democratic transition process than its consolidation process. In addition to its definition, the democratic transition period is more observable in cases of the political system transforming from an authoritarian regime to a more democratically reforming regime with the accompanying constitutional and institutional changes. Political changes are significantly visible to outside observers during the transition period. Practically, democratization is the political reform from a military or one-party regime to a multiparty system, which includes organizing presidential and legislative elections in the final phase of the transition process to choose leaders in the new democratically reformed political system.

Democratic consolidation means that political actors and citizens understand and act by respecting and promoting democratic rule through experience, regular elections, and nationwide dialogue without resorting to violence. How can we measure or analyze the achievement or progress of democratic consolidation related to political consciousness and behavior not only in political society but also in civil society and in the broader population? How to examine or evaluate the process of consolidating democratization and in which conditions or criteria it should be achieved remains ambiguous.

Although three decades have already passed since the dawn of democratization in African countries, more time is needed to conclude the democratization process in Africa. While Western aid donor countries tend to watch and examine in the short term (e.g., 5 or 10 years), no country in global political history, including Western democratically developed countries, has achieved democratization within such a short period. Over the decades or even centuries, countries have experienced countless states of political turmoil, setbacks, and regime turnovers that follow a zigzag path. However, three decades would seemingly be an appropriate period to revisit the first phase of the democratization process.

---

[2] Lindberg (2009, 315–16) mentions, "Most of the contemporary comparative work on democratization is conducted in reference to Dahl's understanding of polyarchy as the minimal but also empirically possible expression of democratic ideals. … I am surprised by that even today, since his list of key explanatory variables includes so many of what the literature still holds as important factors."

2.2.2. Postcolonial Political History and Democratization in Africa

African countries achieved independence after European colonizers gave up their rule. The year 1960 was called "the year of Africa," when 17 African states gained independence. However, this decolonization process did not build a genuine nation-state or democratic governance. Despite the slogan of integrating ethnic groups and regions, the political situation became extremely unstable, and tension arose in struggles for state power among political leaders, regions, and ethnic groups.

After independence, politically incited violence, such as military coups d'état or invasions by rebel forces, became the potential way to seize state power owing to the impossibility of achieving regime turnover through legitimate measures, such as elections. In particular, serious civil wars broke out in Congo and Nigeria in the 1960s that claimed millions of victims.

The interests of powerful Western countries in natural resources often underpinned these civil wars and their continuation. Access to the revenue (rent) from natural resources has been one of the most crucial causes of conflict or civil war in Africa, in addition to the "resource curse" (Auty 1993), which has hindered industrialization and sustainable economic development. In the case of Congo, the mineral resource-rich Katanga province declared its independence in the early 1960s, several years after Congo gained independence. In Nigeria, the Republic of Biafra (Southeastern region), the oil-producing region, declared its independence from the Federal Republic of Nigeria in the mid-1960s.

These postcolonial civil wars dominated the African continent in the first decades after independence, during the most crucial period of the Cold War between the United States and the Soviet Union. Financial, material, and political support from the West and the East to governmental and/or rebel forces made such conflicts more complicated to resolve.

Although African conflicts have often been explained by ethnic rivalries or disputes, a complicated ethnic diversity does not necessarily cause armed conflict. After long struggles over political, economic, historical, social, and cultural interests, ethnicity has been strategically manipulated as a symbol to highlight the "enemy" and clarify the target to attack. Foreign interventions worsened and prolonged the Congolese and Nigerian conflicts in the 1960s.

Before the development of the Washington Consensus, in which major Western donor countries demanded that African countries adopt the multiparty system as a condition of foreign aid (so-called conditionality), Western countries had been willing to support authoritarian regimes in their commercial, diplomatic, and military interests to maintain and expand their influence against communist influence in Africa during the Cold War period. Western countries privileged political stability in African countries because of the threat of regime change brought by revolutionary forces with communist allies. This international situation enabled leaders of African countries to maintain authoritarian regimes, such as a one-party or military regime, until the end of the Cold War. Newly established revolutionary regimes needed close relations with communist regimes, such as the Soviet Union and China. In these fragile authoritarian regimes, violence was the sole means to achieve political turnover.

Table 2.1. Number of successful coups d'état from 1950 to 2022

Number of successful coups d'état	Countries
9	Burkina Faso
6	Benin, Nigeria, Sudan
5	Burundi, Ghana, Mali, Mauritania, Sierra Leone
4	Comoros, Egypt, Guinea Bissau, Niger
3	Central African Republic, Guinea, Lesotho, Togo, Uganda
2	Algeria, Chad, Congo (Rep. of), Democratic Republic of Congo, Ethiopia, Rwanda
1	Côte d'Ivoire, Equatorial Guinea, Eswatini, Gambia, Liberia, Libya, Madagascar, São Tomé, Seychelles, Somalia, Tunisia, Zimbabwe

Source: Duzor and Williamson (2022), simplified and supplemented by the author

During the 1960s and 1970s, frequent military coups d'état occurred as practical means for regime change. Several years after a coup, military leaders were likely to retire from the national army by establishing their own personally customized political party to appeal for so-called normalization of the political process or a return to civilian rule while retaining their power in the army and systematically excluding opponents from the political arena. Politically motivated violence would then repeat this cycle of regime change.

The 1980s are occasionally called the "lost decade" for Africa. The economic situation worsened due to the decline in prices of natural resources, especially oil, in international markets. Despite the massive spending on international aid over the decades, African countries have not achieved the remarkable economic development that donor countries had expected. Western donor countries generally shared a common understanding that the African states had not tackled socio-economic development. In the dramatic transformation in international relations brought about by the end of the Cold War, Western donor countries drastically changed their behavior toward African countries. They began to demand economic and political reforms they perceived as unavoidable, such as privatization, liberalization, and democratization, to improve the governance of African countries.

In addition to the end of the Cold War, we cannot neglect the internal political transformation in each African country. Even after almost three decades of independence, African people could not enjoy political freedom under the (less development-oriented than Asian regimes) authoritarian regimes. African people and civil society struggled for regime change, and economic recession pushed these movements. The late 1980s witnessed storms of demonstrations and protest movements against African governments, calling for a more democratic political regime under a multiparty system.

The end of the Cold War encouraged movements for democratization in Africa for two reasons. The first, mentioned above, was the change in Western donor countries' behavior regarding aid disbursement. The second one was that after the fall of communist regimes, the one-party regimes led by national vanguard parties remarkably lost their legitimacy and raison d'être. The end of the Cold War definitely damaged confidence in the one-party system. After the waves of pressure for democratization, requiring the introduction of the multiparty system, coming from inside and outside each African country, political leaders, who had been mounting stubborn resistance, finally accepted political reform.

2.3. Journey to Democratization in Africa

2.3.1. Dawn of Democratization

The political change or democratization process has not progressed uniquely and straightforwardly in African countries. The political situation has transformed through political and international environmental change. During the democratic transition process in the early 1990s, scholars of African politics were more inclined to focus on which factor was crucial to launching democratization in African countries. They classified internal (domestic) and external (international) factors to analyze the democratic transition.

On the one hand, African leaders faced strong pressure for political reform and liberalization from domestic actors. In the late 1980s, people were frustrated by the inefficiency, corruption, inequality, and violence under Africa's one-party authoritarian regimes. However, the incumbent leaders were neither willing nor capable of reforming national politics by themselves because political liberalization would reduce or end their political domination. Further, while there were enhanced requirements for democratization, new political leaders came from outside political society. Finally, this new political requirement and movement became influential, often recognized as civil society. State leaders had to start negotiating with new (or non-traditional) political forces.

On the other hand, Western donor countries required African countries to adopt democratic reform as the conditionality of foreign aid. Initially, African leaders resisted this pressure from aid donor countries. However, under heavy economic dependence on foreign aid, African leaders could not maintain this resistance for long. Despite their reluctance, authoritarian leaders had to accept political reform.

Regarding the dawn of democratization in African countries, Western scholars tend to focus on international pressures rather than domestic movements to explain the reasons for countries' adoption of democratization. It is easier for outsiders to observe much more visible elements in the change in international circumstances brought by the end of the Cold War, delegitimizing the one-party system and donor countries' pressure by imposing conditionality for foreign aid.

However, as time passed, African countries gradually adopted the multiparty system and began holding regular elections. This requirement from aid donor countries was formally carried out at the institutional level. In addition, several years later, donor countries changed their attitude toward democratization, which had once been part of the conditionality, and decreased their pressure on African countries. Western countries instead started focusing on "good governance," which required a more administration-friendly reform than a troublesome political reform. As the political situation in Africa changed, researchers of African politics shifted their focus from international to domestic factors.

During the initial period of democratization, scholars vigorously discussed which actors had mainly led the democratic transition process in African countries. It was a question of whether the ancient regime leader or a new leader from outside the incumbent political society had the initiative to undertake this democratic transition. It was a focal question about whether democratization would come from above or below.

In the case of democratization from above, which began under the authoritarian leaders' control and allowed them to maintain their political influence until the final stage of democratic transition, the elections were controlled by former regime leaders and merely confirmed their legitimacy. In the case of democratization from above, we could not expect much political progress toward Dahl's concept of polyarchy. However, democratization from above did not occur much in African countries because of the authoritarian leaders' unwillingness to relinquish power voluntarily.

In fact, democratization from below has been broadly observed in African countries. One of the most symbolic democratization-related events from below was the organization of the (Sovereign) National Conference,[3] which principally took place in French-speaking African countries.

The National Conference, inspired by the French Revolution in the late eighteenth century, took place to launch the democratization process. The historical model of the National Conference was the *Convention Nationale* (1792–95). As indicated by the neologism "*Françafrique*," which refers to a particular historical connection and close personal network intertwining political leaders in France and Francophone Africa (former French colonies), these African countries had to share some part of history under the French education system during the period of French colonialism. Ironically, French history (revolution) would continue to haunt political actors during a drastic political change in Francophone African countries.

The National Conference temporarily suspended incumbent state structures, such as the National Assembly, government, and constitution, and ruled during a transitional period under the provisional supreme authority. Its goal was to carry out free and transparent elections to complete the democratic transition after the political institution was changed and reformed. The National Conference introduced its Act (*Acte de Conférence Nationale*) for the transition period as the provisional constitutional law, the High Council of the Republic (*Haut Conseil de la République*)[4] as the temporary legislative organization, and the government of transition.

The National Conference was requested to be organized in francophone African countries as well as Guinea Bissau, Kenya, and Nigeria, even if it did not necessarily occur in these countries (Eboussi Boulaga 1993, 15). Indeed, the National Conference was not necessarily organized in all francophone African countries. In fact, the majority of these countries did not adopt the National Conference or only partially carried out a national dialogue forum without temporarily transferring state sovereignty.[5]

---

[3] On the democratization process launched by the National Conference, see Iwata (2000; 2004).

[4] In Benin, Niger, Togo, and Zaire, it was named Haut Conseil de la République (High Council of the Republic). In Chad, it was named Conseil supérieur de la transition (Transitional Superior Council). In Congo, it was named Conseil supérieur de la République (Superior Council of the Republic). In Gabon, a provisional legislative institution was not established.

[5] In Burkina Faso, Cameroon, Comoros, Guinea, Mauritania, Republic of Central Africa, and Madagascar, presidents rejected the requirement of the National Conference. The government organized a national dialogue forum without transferring state sovereignty to discuss the democratic transition (Du Bois de Gaudusson et al. 1997; 1998).

During the National Conference and democratic transition period, the president's (head of state) executive power was reduced to ceremonial functions, such as signing international treaties and receiving the diplomatic corps. The president performed his function under the transitional government set up through the National Conference. The president had to transfer the personnel management of the army to the prime minister of the transitional government[6] during the transitional period. Representative members of the National Conference from broadly selected organizations were counted from hundreds to more than 2,000 in each organizing country. A prolonged term of the transitional regime would bring a heavy financial burden (Eboussi Boulaga 1993, 12–13).

2.3.2. Challenges and Obstacles in Democratic Transition and Consolidation

Cheeseman (2020) classifies modes of democratic transition (from above, stalemate patterns, from below) and their features and outcomes in Table 2.2. It is not necessarily all democratic trials that follow his patterns. However, this classification helps to grasp the trend and expect potential outcomes of the democratic transition process in African countries.

Table 2.2. African transition trajectories

Mode of Transition	Main Features	Typical Outcome
From above	Limited reform enacted and controlled by the incumbent elite	Incumbent victory, limited openings, and dominant-party state
Stalemate (Externally managed)	Stalemate between warring parties broken by internationally managed peace process and elections	Extremely fragile democratic gains dependent on continued international engagement
Stalemate (Externally triggered)	Stalemate between government and opposition broken by pressure for elections from international actors	Weakly grounded democratic gains, emergence of electoral-authoritarian regimes
Stalemate (Domestically triggered)	Stalemate between government and opposition broken by "corrective coup," paving the way for multipartyism	No immediate gain but greater potential for reform, depending on will of the new ruling junta
Stalemate (Negotiated)	Stalemate between government and opposition leaders broken by elite compromise between moderates from both sides	Protection of core interests of all parties, stable democratic gains
From below	Overwhelming pressure for change led by domestic protest movement	Incumbent defeat, potential for democratic consolidation

Source: Cheeseman (2020, 43)

---

[6] In Congo, the command of the national army was transferred to the prime minister of the transition government (Baniafouna 1995, 51–55).

Since the early 1990s, democratization has not necessarily ensured political freedom and stability in African countries. In extreme cases, several countries experienced armed conflict after political instability and confusion. The Ivorian crisis in the 2000s is an emblematic case of the post-democratization conflict.

In the 1960s–70s, Côte d'Ivoire enjoyed a very positive reputation as the most politically stable African country that was achieving economic growth, called the "Côte d'Ivoire's miracle," under the strong leadership of Houphouët-Boigny and his one-party system with the Democratic Party of Côte d'Ivoire (PDCI). As the wave of democratization rushed toward Côte d'Ivoire, President Houphouët-Boigny attempted democratization from above to sustain his political domination under PDCI, his political machine. Although Côte d'Ivoire introduced the multiparty system in 1990, PDCI remained dominant after the multiparty election. After Houphouët-Boigny died in 1993, Bedié succeeded him and was victorious in the presidential and legislative elections while de facto excluding political opponents, such as Ouattara (former prime minister in the Houphouët-Boigny administration), by manipulating the law (Du Bois de Gaudusson et al. 1997, 263–66). In 1999, Bedié was ousted in a military coup d'état—the first successful regime turnover by a military coup in Côte d'Ivoire's postcolonial history. The military regime led by General Guéï caused political tension due to his electoral fraud. Finally, he was assassinated. Gbagbo, a long-time opposition leader against the PDCI regime, was elected president of the Republic in 2000.

Despite re-establishing the civilian regime, Côte d'Ivoire remained divided by rebel forces (e.g., la force nouvelle) based in the northern region. Peace agreements were repeatedly concluded, such as the Linas–Marcoussi Agreement in 2003, but were repeatedly violated. The Economic Community of West African States (ECOWAS), France, and the African Union dispatched peacekeeping operation forces and staged military interventions in Côte d'Ivoire. After President Gbagbo repeatedly violated the agreement for presidential elections to normalize the political situation, an election eventually took place in 2010. After this presidential election, Côte d'Ivoire again fell into a storm of violence due to Gbagbo's refusal to accept the electoral result and attempt to overturn it. Ouattara declared victory, and the international community recognized his victory and supported his camp. After several months of armed clashes, Gbagbo was arrested in Abidjan. Côte d'Ivoire regained political stability and achieved economic recovery under the Ouattara administration (World Factbook—Cote d'Ivoire, 2022).

The Gambia embraced the multiparty system after winning independence in 1965. However, Jammeh ascended to power through a military coup d'état in 1994. Jammeh kept his personally ruled authoritarian military regime in place under a pseudo-multiparty system while appealing to his self-proclaimed spiritual power to cure patients of HIV/AIDS with bananas (Brisbane Times,

2007). After 22 years of rule of fear, he was over-confident in being re-elected "as programmed" in the presidential election held in December 2016 (World Factbook—The Gambia, 2022). However, Barrow unexpectedly defeated his contender. Similar to Gbagbo, Jammeh refused the result of this election and tried to cancel it. However, he had to accept stepping down under severe pressure from the international community, especially from ECOWAS, with the presence of Senegalese troops sent to the border with the Gambia.

In Niger, the democratic process was initiated from below and seemed to keep advancing after the National Conference through to the first fair election in its postcolonial history. However, Niger's democratic process was reversed by the military coup, which General Baré Maïnassara attempted in 1996 (Du Bois de Gaudusson et al. 1998, 156–60). After three years of his personal rule, he was assassinated in 1999. Tandja was democratically elected in 2000. However, he sought to remove the limitation of the presidential term in 2009, one year before the end of his second (final) term, by modifying the constitution to become de facto president for life. The coup ended Tandja's ambition in 2010. After the transition period, Issoufou was elected president in 2011. In 2021, Bazoum was peacefully elected president (World Factbook—Niger, 2022), and Niger seemed to be returning to democratization. However, General Tchiani attempted his coup with his royalist soldier and detained President Bazoum in 2023 (Melly, 2023). Niger marked the worst record of any African country in undergoing four regime turnovers by military coups d'état since the dawn of democratic transition in the early 1990s.

The international community (practically, Western countries) expected changes in the political system and behavior of political actors through the democratization process—that is, establishing a more democratic political culture to control state resources to escape personal rule, authoritarianism, and nepotism. This subject is related to the concept of democratic consolidation.

In his edited book *Le (non-)renouvellement des elites en Afrique sub-saharienne* (Non-renewal of Elites in Sub-Saharan Africa), Daloz focuses on the political elites' behavior after democratization started. According to Daloz, the generation of political leaders changed through democratization process, but the political behavior of elites did not (Daloz 1999, 19). They maintained their traditions, such as regionalism, clientelism, corruption, the struggle for private interests, personalization of political parties, and instrumentalization of civil society, even after the regime change.

At the dawn of democratization in Africa, this reform was expected to create and spread the democratic culture of political elites and people. A newly (re)introduced democratic system can only be sustained and developed under political actors' fair games and people's continuous dedication to political participation. In the one-party regime, people could not practice the political choice of their own will. Voting was merely a ritual ceremony to re-legitimize the incumbent authoritarian leader and his regime. After democratization started, African people were required to choose their representatives by expressing their own will and responsibility for their choice and acting in democratic engagements in politics. Although certain countries fell into political instability after democratization trials were launched, in general, the governance of African countries has not remarkably worsened (Van de Walle 2003, 306–07). With three decades of experience, we can observe gradual changes in the behavior of political actors and people who neither try nor support seizing power by armed force and think of the country's interests from a long-term perspective, although the political turnover by a military coup has still occurred.

2.4. Evaluations of Africa's Democratization

2.4.1. Positive Views of Democratization

There is no doubt in my mind that Africa has gradually become more politically and economically free over the past almost 20 years and that apart from analyzing the most important causes, this new landscape of institutions, norms, actors, and actions have important effects as well. (Lindberg 2009, 46)

This section examines and reviews the democratization processes and experiences in African countries in the last three decades. Among political scientists, negative perceptions are dominant in evaluating democratization in Africa. However, we cannot dismiss the positive and potential aspects of democratization. This section examines Africa's democratization experiences from both perspectives.

Although pessimistic views on political transformation in Africa in the post-Cold War era broadly dominate among scholars of African politics, peaceful regime turnovers, repeatedly organized elections, and some signs of democratic consolidation have been more frequently and regularly observed, such as in Benin, Ghana, Kenya, Senegal, and South Africa. However, the progression of democratization has not necessarily been straightforward.[7] Indeed, some African countries repeatedly and increasingly experienced elections without any interference from military coups d'état or civil wars. Peaceful regime turnovers through elections are no longer surprising events in the twenty-first

---

[7] Some researchers evaluate the regime change narrowly in the case only where the incumbent head of state or government is defeated in the election. However, this chapter recognizes regime change according to more realistic criteria when a new leader from a political force or party other than the incumbent regime is elected.

century, although certain electoral violence remains a serious concern in African politics.

Elections have regularly taken place in African countries. However, in reality, the sitting president is often likely to win. For instance, from 2007 to 2012, there were 14 changes in top leadership following a nationwide vote, but only three cases (Côte d'Ivoire, Senegal, and Zambia) did an incumbent lose. In another 11 cases, incumbents died in office, reached their term limit, or were ousted in coups prefatory to a new election (Opalo 2012, 83).

Through the regular presidential, legislative, and municipal elections, we can observe the significant change in political behavior, which has become more competitive and democratic in some African countries, though not in all countries on the continent. These peaceful regime transitions and the regular repetition of elections have been relatively freer and fairer than before the democratization process was launched in Africa. The democratic experiences have been accumulated year after year at the continental level, albeit in a non-linear way or often accompanying money politics during the early phases of the democratic transition. These incidents have been observed in the history of democratic transition throughout the world, including in Western countries. However, such a democratization trend in Africa could not be expected until the end of the 1980s. We should recognize that this is remarkable and unignorable progress in African politics.

Since Ghana and Benin launched their democratic reforms, they have each kept a positive reputation as some of Africa's most successful democratization cases. However, their democratization trials have not necessarily been easy.

Even the more pessimistic scholars, who label political reform trials in developing countries as "competitive authoritarianism" and do not recognize a political transformation as democratization, examine Ghana as an exceptional (unexpected) achievement of democratization in Africa. Authors who espouse the competitive authoritarianism theory, who are likely to understand the democratic process in developing countries negatively, mention,

> Ghana's democratization is not explained by our theory. Rather, it was a product of Rawlings's leadership (and, specifically, his investment in credible democratic institutions) and opposition strength. (Levitsky & Way 2010, 307)

Ghana has experienced harsh political events in its postcolonial history. Since winning independence from the United Kingdom in 1957, the Ghanaian people have lived under authoritarian regimes. The founding president and ideological father of Africa's unification, Nkrumah, was ousted by a military coup d'état in 1966. After the first successful attempt, the military coup became the outstanding means for regime change before the dawn of democratization in Ghana. The young military officer, Jerry Rawlings, took power after his second coup attempt in 1981 and led a revolutionary regime.

Rawlings was one of the rare African military leaders who voluntarily accepted the transition to democratization. Ghana faced a difficult economic situation in the 1980s and was required by Western aid donor countries to adopt political reform at the beginning of the 1990s. Given the severe economic crisis and heavy dependence on foreign aid, Ghana had no choice but to accept its democratic transition. The Rawlings administration changed Ghana's constitution by introducing a multiparty political system and allowing opposition parties to enter the political system freely. Rawlings won the first democratically conducted presidential election in Ghana in 1992.

Ghana is also a rare case of an African country that experienced a successful and peaceful democratic transition carried out from above on the incumbent leader's initiative. Since 1992, Ghana has held eight peaceful presidential elections without any suspension of the democratic process by a military coup d'état, and it experienced three regime turnovers through close elections in 2000, 2008, and 2016. Therefore, Ghana exemplifies the hope of democracy in Africa, especially a two-party democracy. It has had one of the most successful democratization processes in Africa. At the same time, Ghana has faced political challenges, such as violence, problematic electoral management, the patronage system, corruption, voting behavior along ethnic and regional lines, and weakness in checking the current power. However, Ghana has not faced any massive post-electoral violence, such as Kenya's post-electoral nationwide violence that occurred in 2007. In its democratization experience, Ghana has improved its electoral management through the National Electoral Commission (NEC), which has tried to maintain its independence from state power (Gyimah-Boadi 2009, 138–49).

We can find some positive signs in Ghanaian politics that the media, civil society, and the NEC have functioned correctly (Jockers et al. 2010, 99–100). Ghana's NEC was established in 1993 and has successfully managed tense elections. The NEC managed and finalized the close presidential elections, in which the incumbents were defeated by their contenders (Gazibo 2020, 180).

Ghana has experienced regime turnovers through elections with significant swings in votes (Jockers et al. 2010, 111). The Ghanaian political situation has significantly improved compared to neighboring countries, such as Côte d'Ivoire, Togo, and Burkina Faso (Jockers et al. 2010, 100).

Benin has experienced as many troublesome political events in its postcolonial history as Ghana. Benin and Ghana have experienced similar political histories at almost the same time. After gaining independence from France in 1960, the Beninese people lived almost entirely under military regimes until 1990. Benin underwent six successful military coups d'état. The last successful coup was directed by Kérékou in 1972. Kérékou led his military-revolutionary regime by adopting Marxism-Leninism and changed the state denomination to the People's Republic of Benin.

However, like Ghana, Benin faced an economic crisis in the 1980s, the lost decade for Africa, and faced strong demands for political reform by domestic civil society organizations in the late 1980s, in addition to the pressure from Western countries. Finally, Kérékou had to accept the organization of the Sovereign National Conference (*La conférence nationale des forces vives de la nation*) by civil society and government organizations in 1990. The National Conference established special transition institutions while reducing President Kérékou's power during the transition period. The transition regime established the new democratic constitutions by organizing a referendum and hosting presidential and parliamentary elections under a multiparty system. Therefore, Benin is one of the most emblematic cases of a peaceful democratic transition from below with civil society forces.

Even three decades after the dawn of democratization, Benin's political institutions established in the democratic transition remain respected and work under democratic rule, although politics is likely conducted by personal networks and regional connections (Cheeseman 2020, 46–47).

The National Autonomous Electoral Commission of Benin (*Commission électorale nationale autonome*, CENA) was established in 1995. It is composed of 23 members representing political parties, often dominated by opposition parties. Despite the confusion and disputes about and within the CENA, it remains a reliable institution for conducting elections in Benin and recognized turnovers of power (in 1996, 2006, and 2016). Gazibo (2020, 180) considers Benin one of Africa's more consolidated democracies.

> While it remains emphatically true that "elections do not equal democracy" — that there is much more to having democracy and making it work than free, fair, and truly competitive elections — it is also the case that institutionalizing free and fair elections, with rigorous and effective electoral administration, is a crucial aspect of democracy. (Diamond 2009, xviii)

> It is of course impossible to conceive of representative democracy without elections. (Lindberg 2009, 6)

Democratization is a political reform that requires a sufficiently long time, sometimes more than half a century, to achieve. Democratization might not necessarily be an appropriate agenda for foreign aid conditionality, which usually targets concluding in a very short term, such as a couple of years. Consequently, we cannot draw a definite conclusion about democratization in Africa after only two or three decades of experience, but we can consider introducing a multiparty democratic system as the beginning of a long political reform road accompanying many turbulent experiences in African countries. However, we have observed pessimistic results and many hopes and progress in democratization in African countries.

Studies on African democratization have been principally based on a Western ideal model. Thus, Western scholars have likely viewed democratization in Africa in comparison with (subtracting from) their own "true" democracy, which has been fostered in the Western world.

In the late 2000s, international circumstances significantly changed the democratization requirements in Africa. The new trend was brought from China. In contrast to traditional Western donor countries, China does not request democratization as a condition of aid for African countries to deliver economic cooperation. This Chinese approach was later called the Beijing Consensus (Alden 2007, 105) in the Western world, in contrast to the Washington Consensus. This approach was welcomed by African leaders, which had received pressure and sanctions from Western donor countries. African countries have tried to establish a close relationship with China. Zimbabwean President Mugabe developed the African "Look East" policy to approach China (Alden 2007, 59).

2.4.2. Negative Views on Democratization

This empirical phenomenon surely contributed to the broad category of "semi-democracy" used in the 1970s and 1980s, giving way to an increasing number of "democracies with adjectives" in the 1990s. (Lindberg 2009, 2)

We have observed positive and negative signs and evaluations of democratization in African countries. In the international community (de facto Western countries), negative views became dominant among scholars of African politics a decade after democratization was launched in African countries.

At the dawn of democratization in the early 1990s, in the post-Cold War era, the international community and Africanist scholars relatively shared an optimistic feeling in political perspectives on Africa's future while occasionally referring to "Africa Renaissance," "rebirth," and "Second Liberalization." However, pessimistic views gradually became dominant a decade after democratization was initiated in African countries (Gyimah-Boadi 2004, 1).

In the late 1990s, Western governments (donors) no longer strongly required democratization and political reform in African countries as aid conditionality. After the 9/11 incident, the United States changed the direction of its African policy by highlighting security issues rather than democratization. European countries also shifted their African policy to more security and refugee issues. In recent decades, emergent donors, such as China and India, have expanded their influence in Africa. These emerging influential partners are unlikely to request political reform in African countries. Economic and diplomatic motives are crucial for these emerging countries to work with/in Africa.

At the dawn of democratization in Africa, France, one of Africa's most influential donor countries at that time, categorically declared its orientation to democratization as its aid conditionality, announced by President Mitterrand at the France–Africa Summit in 1990, which was later called the Declaration of La Baule. However, after a couple of years, France minimized its pressure and support for democratization and returned to its traditional stance to keep its political influence and safeguard its economic interests in Africa, particularly in French-speaking countries. Thus, democratization is no longer at the top of the agenda in the African policy of the Western donor community in the twenty-first century, although rhetoric has remained on its agenda.

As backlash after the high expectations for democratization, pessimistic views and evaluations spread rapidly among Western scholars of African politics. Several years after the political liberalization process started in Africa, political scientists tried to understand the ongoing political reform in African countries by adding adjectives to the word "democracy," such as "semi-," "formal-," "electoral-," "partial-," "weak-," "illiberal-," and "virtual-," to express their reservations concerning political reforms in non-Western regions (Ottaway 2003, 7). Such rhetoric presupposes that democracy exists to some extent. At the same time, there was a common understanding among Western scholars of African politics that "full-" democracy has been established in the Western world.

The majority of negative opinions have been induced by the political reform in Africa in light of phenomena such as electoral fraud, political violence, corruption, limited contribution to economic development, and strained cohabitation in a multi-ethnic society. Scholars viewing African politics pessimistically have understood that the multiparty system neither resolved political problems nor made the behaviors of political actors and people more democratic than donor countries had expected.

One remarkable feature of the democratization process is the increase in money's influence on political life. Money is always an indispensable resource for conducting political activities everywhere. However, it is evident that people speak about money more frequently and openly in African politics compared to the pre-democratization time.[8]

---

[8] Ghana has maintained its positive reputation for democratization as a "star pupil" in Africa in the eyes of the international community since the 1990s (Lindberg 2010, 132). According to Lindberg's case studies on Ghana, expenditures on electoral campaigns have increased. For example, in the parliamentary election campaigns, a candidate consumed USD 3,000 in 1996, 10,000 in 2000, 40,000 in 2004, and 75,000 in 2008, with the most

During the early years after democratization launched, money was likely to be considered a more essential and powerful tool in political games. Political actors faced more severe competition compared to the one-party authoritarian regime era. They needed to spend more money or other resources on electoral campaigns in order to win the more "democratic" elections. It is likely that the international community would criticize such a situation as corruption.

However, such a scenario might be called the first initiation of democratization, instead of the rule of armed forces, violence, or mobilization by the army and dominant party under a one-party regime. While state violence became less influential, money began talking more powerfully in the political arena during the initial years after democratization. This phenomenon is not only related to African and new democracies but has been universal, including throughout the first and second waves of democratization in Western countries.

Although scholars of political science have not been willing to highlight money in the electoral process in a political transition, no election can take place without money, not only for holding the election but also for running electoral campaigns. Money is the indispensable gasoline of politics, and it talks much more directly in the first elections during a political transition period, which is not unique to Africa.

> A large number of political regimes in the contemporary world... have established the institutional façades of democracy, including regular multiparty elections for the chief executive, in order to conceal (and reproduce) harsh realities of authoritarian governance. Although in historical perspective the authoritarian use of elections is nothing new, contemporary electoral authoritarian regimes take the time-honored practice of electoral manipulation to new heights. (Schedler 2006, 1)

After countless attempts to examine and interpret the democratization process and cases in Africa by limiting its meaning to the use of particular adjectives, many Western scholars studying African politics have gradually abandoned the concept of democratization or democracy. Instead, they have adopted the idea of "renewed" authoritarianism, adding an adjective for precision or to distinguish their understanding of the political process from "traditional

---

expensive campaign on record estimated by the candidate at 600,000. Members of parliament need to print more T-shirts in campaigns not only for their election staff but also for ordinary voters in the constituency and offer personal assistance to maintain their influence. T-shirts might be considered an important item by politicians to attract voters (Lindberg 2010, 124). The author once asked someone why people wear T-shirts displaying a candidate's face. She said, "It is a free T-shirt," not because she supports this candidate. The increasing role of money in politics is generally acknowledged, even though this trend is more remarkable among ministers and presidential candidates than ordinary parliamentarians.

(old)" authoritarianism to understand the political process in African countries in the post-Cold War era.

As time has passed since the political liberalization reform started, pessimistic views on political transition have spread among scholars of African political studies. Concepts derived from authoritarianism have expanded their influence in the study of African politics. For instance, "semi-authoritarianism," "electoral authoritarianism," or "competitive authoritarianism" have been some of the most repeated "nuanced" concepts based on authoritarianism related to the political process in Africa since the 1990s.

Ottaway (2003) highlights the semi-authoritarianism concept in *Democracy Challenged*. Semi-authoritarianism does not mean a failed democracy. It is a controlled condition of democracy that the regime adopts to prevent competitive democracy with a formal "democratic" system, such as the multiparty system.

According to Ottaway, the political situation in developing countries is not based on democracy but on authoritarianism. "Semi-authoritarianism" is no longer a type of democracy but a different political category. The characteristics of semi-authoritarianism are the "transfer of power through controlled election," "weak political institutionalization," "gap between political and economic reform," and "limitation of civil society" (Ottaway 2003, 15–19). The semi-authoritarian regime is a political hybrid with no political competition to seek power. However, minimal political space, such as political parties, civil society, and the press, is permitted (Ottaway 2003, 3).

> Electoral authoritarian regimes play the game of multiparty elections by holding regular elections for the chief executive and a national legislative assembly. Yet they violate the liberal-democratic principles of freedom and fairness so profoundly and systematically as to render elections instruments of authoritarian rule rather than "instruments of democracy." Under electoral authoritarian rule, elections are broadly inclusive (they are held under universal suffrage) as well as minimally pluralistic (opposition parties are allowed to run), minimally competitive (opposition parties, while denied victory, are allowed to win votes and seats), and minimally open (opposition parties are not subject to massive repression, although they may experience repressive treatment in selective and intermittent ways). (Schedler 2006, 3)

The concept of electoral authoritarianism highlights elections deployed in an authoritarian style. In electoral authoritarianism, elections are institutionalized and take place regularly but are controlled and manipulated by the authoritarian regime with accompanying electoral fraud or restriction of the opposition's participation to ensure a comfortable result in favor of the incumbent regime. Although this is distinguished from democracy and full authoritarianism, regime turnover is not expected through elections under the electoral authoritarian regime.

> Unlike authoritarian regimes that permit limited forms of pluralism in civil society, EA (electoral authoritarian) regimes go a step further and open up political society (the party system) as well to limited forms of pluralism. (Schedler 2006, 5)

According to Schedler (2006), minimal civil liberty is ensured for the activities of civil society under the electoral authoritarian regime, although political turnover cannot be expected through civil society's interventions and elections.

In recent years, the idea of competitive authoritarianism has influenced political scientists to gain a better understanding of the political process experienced in developing countries in the post-Cold War era.

Levitsky and Way (2010) distinguish competitive authoritarian regimes from full authoritarian and full democracy regimes. They classify the political regime in most developing or non-Western countries as a "competitive authoritarian regime" while broadly covering its range and strictly limiting the range of full-authoritarian regimes and full democracy:

> Competitive authoritarian regimes are distinguished from full authoritarianism in that constitutional channels exist through which opposition groups compete in a meaningful way for executive power. Elections are held regularly and opposition parties are not legally barred from contesting them. Opposition activity is above ground: Opposition parties can open offices, recruit candidates, and organize campaigns, and politicians are rarely exiled or imprisoned. In short, democratic procedures are sufficiently meaningful for opposition groups to take them seriously as arenas through which to contest for power.
> What distinguishes competitive authoritarianism from democracy, however, is the fact that incumbent abuse of the state violates at least one of three defining attributes of democracy: (1) free elections, (2) broad protection of civil liberties, and (3) a reasonably level playing field. (Levitsky & Way 2010, 7)

According to Levitsky and Way, as well as other scholars highlighting the concept of authoritarianism, it is not appropriate to adopt the concept of democracy to understand the political transformation of a hybrid regime in non-Western countries and regions after the end of the Cold War, but better to understand this as a subtype of renewed authoritarianism.

> Rather than "partial," "incomplete," or "unconsolidated" democracies, these cases should be conceptualized for what they are: a distinct, nondemocratic regime type. Instead of assuming that such regimes are

in transition to democracy, it is more useful to ask why some democratized and others did not. This is the goal of our study. (Levitsky & Way 2010, 4)

According to Levitsky and Way, under competitive authoritarian regimes, relatively competitive elections regularly occur in which opposition parties and candidates can participate without bare exclusions of opposition and severe fraud orchestrated by the authority. However, these elections are not entirely free and fair while skewing the rule and field to limit opponents' opportunities to sustain the incumbent regime's dominance (Levitsky & Way 2010, 8).

Levitsky and Way propose three indicators (Western linkage, organizational power, and Western leverage) to measure and classify political regimes in the post-Cold War era, distinguishing competitive authoritarian regimes from full authoritarian regimes and full democracy. They consider that non-Western countries would become more democratic when Western linkage and leverage are strong; in other words, the Western influence is strong. When the (domestic) political and executive power is strong, these countries will likely become more authoritarian.

Table 2.3. Predicted and actual regime outcomes in Sub-Saharan Africa, 1990–2008

Case	Linkage	Organizational Power	Leverage	Predicted Outcome	Actual Outcome
Benin	Low	Low	High	Unstable Authoritarianism	Democratization
Botswana	Low	High	High	Stable Authoritarianism	Stable Authoritarianism
Cameroon	Low	Medium	Medium	Stable Authoritarianism	Stable Authoritarianism
Gabon	Low	High	Medium	Stable Authoritarianism	Stable Authoritarianism
Ghana	Low	Medium	High	Unstable Authoritarianism	Democratization
Kenya	Low	Medium	High	Unstable Authoritarianism	Unstable Authoritarianism
Madagascar	Low	Low	High	Unstable Authoritarianism	Unstable Authoritarianism
Malawi	Low	Low	High	Unstable Authoritarianism	Unstable Authoritarianism
Mali	Low	Low	High	Unstable Authoritarianism	Democratization
Mozambique	Low	Medium High	High	Stable Authoritarianism	Stable Authoritarianism
Senegal	Low	Medium	High	Unstable Authoritarianism	Unstable Authoritarianism
Tanzania	Low	Medium High	High	Stable Authoritarianism	Stable Authoritarianism
Zambia	Low	Medium Low	High	Unstable Authoritarianism	Unstable Authoritarianism
Zimbabwe	Low	High	High	Stable Authoritarianism	Stable Authoritarianism

Source: Levitsky and Way (2010, 306)

These authors over-evaluate Western influence (linkage and leverage) on the political transformation of developing countries. Western countries did not promote political liberalization in their foreign policy toward the Third World in the Cold War era but thoroughly supported authoritarian regimes to enlarge Western alliances against the Soviet Bloc. Even after the Cold War ended, political liberalization was not the principal objective of their African policy. We need to be careful about the flexibility of the behavior of Western countries toward political development or liberalization.

Western aid donors have been inclined to require a clearly visible change and judge the result of the political transformation in the short term, such as five years or so. Moreover, these countries have evaluated the democratic process in Africa and other developing regions from a perspective based on an imagined model of democratization.

Democratization is a political reform, not a magical panacea that resolves all political problems by simultaneously bringing economic development to developing countries. Western countries underwent the same long, non-linear process earlier. They are prone to easily put aside their own experiences of long and painful history when they require the democratization of others. No Western country carried out this painstaking reform within five years or even a decade. African countries also need sufficient time and patience to digest democratic reform according to their economic, political, and social contexts.

2.5. Conclusion

There is an understandable temptation to load too many expectations on this concept and to imagine that by attaining democracy, a society will have resolved all of its political, social, economic, administrative, and cultural problems. Unfortunately, "all good things do not necessarily go together." (Schmitter & Karl 2009, 13)

This chapter traced and examined the democratization process and experiences in African countries. This is one of the most crucial challenges for political development in Africa.

In the early 1990s, aid donor countries straightforwardly required political reform; in other words, democratization presupposed that political liberation would bring economic development and administrative efficiency to African countries. However, democratization has not automatically resolved all political, economic, administrative, and cultural problems (Schmitter & Karl 2009, 13–15).

Despite various negative evaluations or analyses, democratization has certainly brought about critical political changes and improvements, such as peaceful regime change through relatively freer and fairer elections, even with some irregularities due to lack of experience; enlargement of freedom of the press, which has improved political transparency; and active political involvement in civil society.

Democratization redrew blurred boundaries among Africa's political regimes between democratizing and authoritarian countries. We have observed multiple peaceful regime turnovers through elections in African countries like Benin, Ghana, Kenya, Senegal, and Zambia since the 1990s. Indeed, these positive phenomena are not necessarily observed in all African countries. In some countries, we should recognize the completely opposite realities working against democratization, such as in Angola, Central African Republic, Democratic Republic of Congo, Equatorial Guinea, and many other countries. It is not difficult to point out and criticize visible problems or violations of democratic rules during three decades of African democratization trials. However, these pessimistic visions often neglect various positive political changes and progress.

In conclusion, political development does not necessarily bring economic development in the short term. We do not find any direct correlation between political and economic development as aid donors expected or forced on aid recipient countries at the beginning of the post-Cold War era. Economic development in African countries in the twenty-first century is a more appropriate case. This still heavily depends on the rising prices of natural resources. Engagements and efforts for democratization do not necessarily bring GDP growth in the very short term. However, trials and experiences of democratization improve the business environment, which makes business more competitive and creates a more transparent society in the long term. Freedom of expression should not be ignorable to conduct business freely.

Democratization is not a political reform that can be fully achieved within a couple of years or even one or two decades. Undergoing this process requires sufficient and appropriate time, depending on each country's historical, social, and political contexts. In addition, African countries continue to tackle enormous challenges in state- and nation-building after around a half-century of their history as sovereign states. Meanwhile, these African countries have been required by the international community (aid donor countries) to simultaneously carry out democratization and economic development for decades. In world political history, it must be the toughest challenge, which not all countries have faced. It takes a sufficiently appropriate amount of time to complete democratization; there are no shortcuts.

We must keep carefully watching Africa's democratization in the longer term while keeping a critical eye but not necessarily a pessimistic view.

Chapter 3

Political Impact of Decentralization in Africa: Redrawing Boundaries in Local Politics[1]

3.1 Introduction

Over the past three decades, the political and administrative boundaries have significantly changed and been redrawn between international organizations, central governments, and local governments. Globalization somehow relativized state sovereignty in the world economy. Decentralization encouraged the local government's initiative for efficient management by redefining its relationships with the central government and international community. Decentralization in the globalization era promised a more direct connection between the local government (people) and the world beyond the central government's intermediary. However, decentralization has not necessarily reduced the state's authority dramatically in Africa as we expected but activated local politics, redrawing boundaries in national and local politics and creating political dramas in African localities. After decentralization was launched, local politics provided more political opportunities for local leaders and became a harsher political battlefield.

What have been the effects of decentralization on African politics since the decentralization process began in the mid-1990s? In recent years, decentralization (accompanied by rapid urbanization) has been an outstanding phenomenon in African countries and has had significant effects on African societies, from the people's everyday lives to governance at the local and state levels. Urbanization has amplified the impact of decentralization on the governance of African countries. Decentralization and urbanization have also expanded the economic and political gaps (boundaries) between urban and rural local governments as devolution has progressed from the central to local governments. Decentralization encourages international cooperation between African and non-African local governments and among African local governments (called

---

[1] This chapter was originally published in the journal of the International Studies Association of Ritsumeikan University (Kyoto, Japan): Iwata, T. (2018). Political impact of decentralization in Africa. *Ritsumeikan Annual Review of International Studies, 17*, 1–25.

la coopération décentralisée in Francophone countries, hereinafter "decentralized cooperation").

Furthermore, decentralization has significantly influenced the local politics and behavior of local (political) actors, and it may change the relationship between the central government and local governments and between a local government and its residents. The political influence of elected mayors of big cities (i.e., not appointed by the state authority), especially in the capital cities, has strengthened as decentralization has progressed to its full scale. Although decentralization has had significant political effects in African countries, it has not been sufficiently studied in investigations into African politics. Decentralization has been principally focused on the issue of administrative reform while neglecting political dynamism or struggles. Thus, this chapter highlights the political impact of decentralization on African countries by focusing on local governments in the context of rapid, ongoing urbanization.

First, this chapter traces the brief history of the contemporary decentralization process in Africa. Second, it reflects on the effects of decentralization on post-electoral African politics[2] and international relations by examining local elections, decentralized cooperation, and political dramas in the local governments in Benin and Burkina Faso.

3.2. Decentralization Process in African Countries

3.2.1. Overview of Decentralization in Africa

Decentralization is generally defined as the process of financial, human, and technical devolution from the central government to local governments to empower local governance. In Africa, decentralization reforms began in the mid-1990s as a condition for receiving foreign aid from Western donor countries to carry out "good governance."

Since independence, almost all African countries have had more or less authoritarian regimes at their helm. Such one-party or military regimes have endeavored to maximally centralize the political control under the central government (or in the leader's hands) to ensure and maintain economic, political, and social dominance.

African countries have experienced decentralization through two decades of political and administrative reforms, and this decentralization has had significant political effects on local politics. Insofar as the devolution process progressed,

---

[2] The author has previously studied the effects of decentralization on elections in Benin by examining three consecutive elections (Presidential 2006, Legislative 2007, Municipal 2008) after decentralization was initiated (Iwata 2011).

local governments in African countries have expanded their direct international cooperation with foreign local (and central) governments. Thus, decentralization has included African local governments in the globalizing world (Iwata 2012a, 145).

While Western countries initially requested this contemporary decentralization process as a means of carrying out "administrative" reform, decentralization did not remain an administrative reform; as the devolution process progressed, it exposed its political effects on African countries. In general, more local representatives were elected in basic local governments after the decentralization process took place, in contrast to some local representatives (e.g., the governor of a supervising local government body) that are still appointed by the state authority. Thus, the progress of decentralization has raised questions about democratization (Iwata 2012a, 146).

Decentralization significantly stimulated the international activities of African local governments working with foreign local governments because devolution allowed the local governments to actively undertake international cooperation activities (Iwata 2012a, 147). Decentralized cooperation brought about a new political dynamism and momentum in African localities. The decentralization reform was aimed at redefining the roles and responsibilities not only of the central government but also of local governments. In other words, essentially, decentralization has been a political reform (Saito 2008, 284).

When the decentralization process started in African countries, Western donor countries presumed that it would improve the quality of local governance. Furthermore, these Western donor countries seemed to naïvely expect that decentralization would foster democratization from local governance to national politics (Iwata 2016a, 10–11).

Although the process of decentralization has occurred according to the unique socio-political situation in each African country, we can find commonality in its initiation as a requirement for receiving foreign aid. In contrast to democratization reforms, African governments have not faced strong pressure for decentralization from the people or civil society. Moreover, decentralization seemed to be a less (politically) risky "administrative" reform for authoritarian African leaders because it was unlikely to threaten their political dominance, at least in the short term. Therefore, many authoritarian African leaders have been willing to accept the requirement of decentralization reform and show their positive involvement in "good governance" because the Western donor countries have not seriously required democratization as a condition for receiving aid.

Before the 1990s (the dawn of democratization), African governments had already taken place a "deconcentration" reform of local governance without any significant devolution of executive power or financial and human resources.

Therefore, the transfer of power and resources from the central government to local governments is a crucial issue in decentralization. However, democratization is an inseparable factor in considering and evaluating decentralization. Often, foreign aid has been derived from the naïve idea that decentralization will install local democracy in African countries rather than being based on the real experiences or historicity of Africa (Iwata 2012a, 146–47).

3.2.2. Brief History of Politics and Decentralization in Benin and Burkina Faso

This part briefly traces the history of politics and decentralization in Benin and Burkina Faso.[3] Over the last two decades, Benin has been seen as a model of democratization in Africa by the international community.[4] However, Benin experienced political storms in its first 30 years after independence and until the dawn of democratization.[5]

After three decades of authoritarian regimes (including a pseudo-Marxist-Leninist revolutionary regime), in the late 1980s, teachers, students, and labor unionists repeatedly and increasingly held protest demonstrations demanding the resignation of President Kérékou. In 1990, the first Sovereign National Conference (*Conférence nationale des forces de vive de la nation*; Iwata 2000; 2004) took place to launch democratization without bloodshed.[6]

According to the new Constitution, *Etats généraux de l'administration territoriale* (Forum for Administrative Reform) was held in 1993 with the aim of realizing the reorganization of the local government structure and reforming Benin's local administrative bodies from districts and sub-districts (*sous-préfectures*) to "*communes*" as the basic local government bodies. Seventy-seven communes

---

[3] This chapter examines the cases in Burkina Faso before the regime turnover caused by the military coup d'état of 2022, ousting President Koboré, in order to highlight the political impacts of decentralization in Africa.

[4] After the democratization process started, Benin had six presidential elections, six National Assembly elections, and three local elections with no suspension caused by the military coup or civil war.

[5] For the first 12 years after its independence in 1960, Benin had six regime changes resulting from military coups. Finally, the Marxist-Leninist military regime led by Kérékou held office for 17 years (October 1972–February 1990). Meanwhile, political freedom was strictly limited, and the national economy was heavily degraded.

[6] After a one-year transition period, the Seventh Constitution was adopted through a referendum in December 1990. The presidential election, the first free election after independence, took place in March 1991.

were established as the main actors in local development through a devolution from the central government (Iwata 2011, 101).

After introducing decentralization-related laws and institutions, local elections took place, enabling local residents to choose their local representatives directly, "*les conseillers de conseil de commune*" (the councilors of the Commune Council).[7] The mayor (*le maire*), the head of the commune, is indirectly elected by the councilors themselves. The mayor is also the concurrent chairperson of the Commune Council (Iwata 2011, 101).[8]

Like Benin, Burkina Faso's political history has experienced considerable turbulence since independence. After having experienced repeated regime turnovers through military coups d'état, the revolutionary regime (1983–87) led by young military officers such as Sankara and Compaoré came to power. Compaoré became head of state after the military coup in 1987, killing his elder comrade, President Sankara, and he retained power for 27 years. Although Compaoré's Burkina Faso had been recognized as one of the most authoritarian and stable regimes in Africa, he was unexpectedly easily ousted. At the end of October 2014, two days of the popular insurgency, which followed demonstrations conducted by opposition parties and civil society over weeks, mobilized half a million people across the country, who were protesting Compaoré's attempt to enact constitutional change to ensure his presidency for life. This insurgency ended Compaoré's regime (Iwata 2016b, 147–48).[9]

Even under authoritarian rule, the Compaoré administration attracted significant attention from Western donor countries (especially France and Germany) and developed a positive reputation as the model of decentralization and decentralized cooperation among the French-speaking West African countries.

The decentralization process in Burkina Faso started in 1995. Under the Local Government Act of 2004, the legal framework for decentralization was established, and 359 communes (including eight wards in Bobo-Dioulasso and Ouagadougou,

---

[7] The number of councilors (9–49) is determined according to the population size of the commune.

[8] In addition, the 12 regional administrative units, the "*Départements*" (prefectures), were established. The role of a prefecture is to coordinate with the communes and the central government. The prefecture maintains a superiority of functions in terms of the supervision (*tutelle*) of commune administration, while the central government continues to assign a "*Préfet*" (i.e., the Governor of the Département).

[9] Due to the nationwide popular insurgencies and military revolt, President Compaoré resigned and escaped to neighboring Côte d'Ivoire, escorted by French troops. France and the United States fervently supported Compaoré in the interest of ensuring regional security in West Africa under the threat of armed jihadist groups.

cities with special status) were set up as basic local government bodies. In addition, 13 municipalities (*régions*) were established as the supervising bodies of communes. In 2006, municipal elections, which were the first ever since the full implementation of decentralization, took place to elect commune councilors. After the election, mayors were selected among the elected councilors.

After Compaoré was *de facto* ousted from power in 2014, decentralization-related institutions and local governments (communes) were immediately suspended and then dissolved.[10] The transitional government sent governors to temporarily govern local government bodies until new local representatives could be installed in municipal elections held under the new regime (Iwata 2016a, 23). After one year of rule under the transitional government, presidential and legislative elections took place in November 2015 after a failed coup attempt two months earlier by the special armed forces (*Régiment spécial présidentiel*, RSP) supporting former President Compaoré. Subsequently, municipal elections took place in May 2016.

3-3. Political Impact of Decentralization

3.3.1. Local Governance under Decentralization

Decentralization inevitably activated local politics in African countries, thereby enhancing the politicization of local governance. Before decentralization started in African countries, politics had generally been focused on political issues in the capital city, as indicated by an examination of various incidents, from military coups d'état to democratization. However, local politics is no longer a negligible subject in understanding the situation of African politics, even at the national level, as decentralization continues to progress to its full scale.

As devolution gradually progressed, the political influence of elected local leaders, especially mayors, over their localities increased. Today, mayors can more directly mobilize financial and human resources in their constituencies rather than relying on members of (national) parliament. As decentralization continues to progress, the status of mayor is becoming more attractive to, and crucial for, ambitious politicians to achieve their political goals. Accordingly, decentralization significantly stimulates local politics. We can observe what Bayart pointed out as "the politics of the belly" (*la politique du ventre*) and

---

[10] The positions of mayors and councilors of the communes were dissolved by the transitional government to eradicate the influence of the former regime as well as the National Assembly, as the representatives of the local governments (the Commune Council) were dominated by the Congress for Democracy and Progress (CDP, *le Congrès pour la démocratie et le progrès*), the dominant party founded by Compaoré (Iwata 2016a, 23).

"extraversion" in local politics in Africa as well as national politics (quoted in Iwata 2012a, 149–50).

The political reactivation brought about by decentralization exposed the political revival of local or traditional authorities. Invariably, (re-)election depends on local leaders being locally recognized, prominent people (*fils de terroir*), or individuals who can attract massive support by virtue of being traditionally prestigious personalities in the locality. Their local authority and political influence often derive from traditional chieftaincy. It is quite significant that decentralization as a modern administrative reform made the traditional authorities more politically influential in the decision-making and electoral processes in African local governance (Iwata 2012a, 150).

Thus, decentralization has significantly affected the political power balance in local communities (Iwata 2011). However, a few researchers have focused on the political impact of decentralization on elections because few African countries have had repeated local elections since the establishment of full decentralization. Decentralization stimulated the international activities of local governments (decentralized cooperation) in Africa. Newly elected representatives in the local governments face many requirements from residents regarding local development and individual requests. African local governments needed to establish international cooperation with foreign local governments to supplement resources because of the central government's lack of financial, human, and technical devolution (Iwata 2016a, 11).

Figure 3.1. Request from the National Association of Local Governments of Benin for increasing financial devolution

Source: Author (February 2017, Cotonou, Benin)

In 2017, 77 communes (the total number of basic local governments) were allocated only 4% of the whole national budget in Benin.[11] The National Association of Communes of Benin (*Association Nationale des Communes du Bénin*, ANCB) has repeatedly requested that the central government authorize financial devolution of up to 15% of the national budget. Under the current conditions, only the big urban local governments can afford to invest in and manage local development.

In some African countries where democracy is taking root, local elections have become more crucial in the political scene, even in national politics. Local elections can even affect the next presidential election. In addition, decentralization with devolution has increased the political presence of the mayor. This is a sign of the political transformation taking place between the local governments and the central government through the growing interest of the residents. Mayors, for example, have been discharged one after another due to political disputes among the councilors of the communes. In Benin, the Commune Councils have dismissed tens of mayors since decentralization was launched (Iwata 2011, 104–05).

3.3.2. Elections in the Decentralization Era

Benin stipulated decentralization-related laws to complete the decentralization process. The local government bodies were restructured into 77 communes and 12 *département* (prefectures) through the decentralization process. The *conseillers* (councilors) of the commune, the representatives of local government (Commune Council), are directly elected by the residents of each commune-based constituency. After local elections take place, the elected councilors select their mayor from the Commune Council, although the governor of the prefecture is still appointed by the central government as the supervisor of communes. In terms of political influence, the power of (elected) mayors had become stronger than before decentralization started (Iwata 2012a, 148).

As the decentralization process progressed, the costs for politicians to be (re-)elected increased considerably. Politics of the belly (*la politique du ventre*) became more visible in local politics. The development projects in communes became more politicized. In Benin, as well as in other French-speaking African countries, local elections take place in a proportional system, not in a majoritarian system. Local elections have become a battlefield for the short-term economic interests of politicians and residents (Iwata 2012a, 152).

---

[11] Interview with Mr. Kpatcha, Secretary of Abomey commune, in charge of decentralized cooperation (March 1, 2017, Cotonou, Benin). According to the national budget of 2017 (2.01 trillion CFA francs) (Benin To Info, January 7, 2017), the local budget might be about 80 billion CFA francs (USD 130 million) for all 77 communes.

Meanwhile, when the "official" electoral campaign is launched, the real "electoral campaign in the night" occurs. This refers to the practice where candidate supporters visit the residents in their constituency at their homes to buy their votes, proposing rice bags or cash (from 1,000 to 5,000 FCFA, which is about USD 2 to 10, depending on the status of the targeted person). Such an act is also called *"achat de conscience"* (buying the spirit) in Benin. Although violent, deadly clashes between supporter groups still occur, violence is no longer a decisive factor in the current elections in Benin (Iwata 2011, 104).

Moreover, the progress of decentralization has made fund-raising for the local elections more crucial. Hence, even in local elections, the politics of the belly became a more visible phenomenon. During electoral campaigns, expressions such as "buying the spirit" or "a mouth that is eating does not talk" (*La bouche qui mange ne parle pas*) (Métodjo 2008, 148) become more widespread in communities.

Furthermore, the local administration has been undertaken in a more politicized manner since decentralization started on a full scale. The politicization of local elections has made post-electoral local governance more fragile.

3.4. Development of Local Governments' International Cooperation

3.4.1. Decentralized Cooperation amid Globalization

Decentralized cooperation has expanded in African countries as the decentralization process has advanced. One crucial motive of decentralized cooperation is insufficient financial, human, and technical devolution from the central government to local governments (Dangnon 2009, 146–47). Thus, many African local governments seek to supplement these resources through direct cooperation agreements with foreign (local) governments to respond to residents' requests and to promote the interests of the local political leader (Iwata 2012a, 153).

According to the French government, decentralized cooperation (*coopération décentralisée*) is the framework of international cooperation for local governments with foreign/domestic local partners in order to carry out common objectives (Foreign Ministry of France 2007).

Coopération décentralisée is the ensemble of actions for international cooperation with an agreement on the objectives of common interest between French and foreign local governments. Coopération décentralisée takes place in diverse forms such as sister-city, development programs, and technical exchange. Coopération décentralisée is speculated in the largest framework of local government's foreign action by the circular of Prime Minister, announced on May 26, 1983.[12]

The French government has thoroughly promoted decentralized cooperation, encouraging the local governments of France and other European donor countries, such as Germany, Italy, and Switzerland, to participate in cooperation projects with Francophone African local governments[13] (Iwata 2016a, 11).

The French government is keen to maintain its influence over the former African colonies at the (inter-)national and local levels. Decentralized cooperation might be a local version of *Françafrique*.[14] Burkina Faso is geopolitically crucial for France because of its location at the center of French-speaking West African countries. Therefore, France was eager to bolster Burkina Faso as the model of decentralized cooperation in Africa.

(Politically) ambitious mayors are keen to promote their political influence through decentralized cooperation. After decentralization started, the mayors of big local governments began to travel abroad more frequently. However, decentralized cooperation unsurprisingly expanded the gap in terms of international cooperation between big urban local governments and small rural ones, because the urban local governments are more likely to attract foreign partners' attention (Iwata 2012a, 154). In addition, decentralized cooperation makes local residents more conscious of the political situation in their country through direct communication in comparison to foreign local partners.

---

[12] French Ministry of the Interior & Ministry of Foreign Affairs. (2011). Circular of April 20, 2001, on decentralized cooperation of French local authorities and their groups with foreign local authorities and their groups (*Circulaire du 20 avril 2001 sur la coopération décentralisée des collectivités territoriales françaises et de leurs groupements avec des collectivités territoriales étrangères et leurs groupements*). https://www.senat.fr/ct/ct04-02/ct04-0228.html (accessed September 20, 2023).

[13] France is an aggressive promoter of decentralized cooperation in Africa (principally in Francophone Africa). Decentralized cooperation is not only a cooperation tool but also a "value" for European countries that is based on their experience of reconciliation after World War II. Decentralized cooperation was launched between French and German local governments to establish a multilateral network of two nations for sustainable peace. Furthermore, decentralized cooperation was developed through the integration process of the European Union. Decentralized cooperation is literally cooperation among local governments and is not limited to cultural exchange within the sister-city framework. Decentralized cooperation was stimulated and expanded through the decentralization process, which enabled local governments to pursue more direct and international cooperation with foreign local governments in pursuit of promoting local interests.

[14] Verschave (2000).

Africités (*Africities*) is the largest pan-African summit of local governments. Africités is authorized by the *United Cities and Local Government* (UCLG) and its African headquarters. The first Africités was held in 1998 in Abidjan. The fifth conference was held in Marrakesh in 2009.[15] This summit received 3,600 participants from 72 countries. Africités has become an important arena for diplomacy among African local governments.

3.4.2. Politicization of Decentralized Cooperation

Indeed, decentralization has had a political impact in African countries and societies with the revival of traditional authorities in this modernized local governance. Decentralization made local governance more politicized and globalized through decentralized cooperation in the midst of competition for accessing additional resources. We can acknowledge the case of Abomey (Benin) as one of the most symbolic cases to describe the political impact of decentralization on African local governance.

The commune of Abomey (located 160 km north of Cotonou, the economic capital of Benin) was the heart of the Dahomey Kingdom before French colonial rule started. The Dahomey Kingdom expanded its territory through wars against neighboring kingdoms or communities, while the slave trade flourished and strongly resisted the French invasion through armed struggles in the late nineteenth century. Abomey is not only important for its historical legacy but also for tourism, as its imperial palaces were declared UNESCO world cultural heritage sites.

As previously mentioned, it is indispensable to be a prominent local personality or to receive support from such an individual to become the local government's leader. In a city established by a precolonial kingdom, such as Abomey, such individuals are indispensable. As his family name indicates, Mr. Blaise Glèlè-Ahanhanzo, Mayor of Abomey, is a descendant of King Glèlè, who ruled Dahomey in the mid-nineteenth century (1858–89), the most prosperous era in the kingdom's history. Thus, he symbolizes the decentralization of Benin and has profited remarkably from the decentralized cooperation while increasing

---

[15] At the Marrakesh summit, it is noteworthy that the declaration on triangle local cooperation among Chinese–French–African local governments was pronounced at the end of this summit in the presence of Mr. Chen Haosu, President of the Chinese–African People's Friendship Association (CAPFA) with Cités Unies France (CUF). It seemed to commence a new phase in decentralized cooperation in Africa. Despite technical difficulties and cultural differences, it is a significant landscape change in international cooperation among local governments. The CUF is the counterpart organization of the Chinese–African People's Friendship Association. This tri-party local cooperation surprised the world, but it was not an accident for China and France, as the CAPFA and the CUF had already struck an agreement on Africa's development in 2007 (CUF 2007).

his "political capital" in Bourdieu's sense (Iwata 2012a, 155). He has been energetically involved in local diplomacy while seeking to attract foreign local partners and foreign aid agencies by emphasizing Abomey's historical legacy.

Figure 3.2. Interview with the Mayor of Abomey

Source: Author (October 2005, Cotonou, Benin)

He was not satisfied with the traditional French local partner, the commune of Albi (a small local government in southern France), and tried to expand Abomey's international cooperation. He also established individual contacts with aid agencies, such as DANIDA (The Danish International Development Agency) and JICA (The Japan International Cooperation Agency), and concluded a cooperation agreement with Asian local governments, such as Gwangju (South Korea) in 2010 and Zibo (China) in 2017. This was the second case of a Beninese local government establishing direct cooperation with a Chinese local government after the agreement was reached between Cotonou and Ningbo (China) and the first case of establishing one with a Korean local government. The Mayor of Abomey is one of few mayors in Benin who could meet the U.S. and Chinese ambassadors to Benin. His historical and royal family legacy significantly helped his prominent local diplomacy.

Decentralized cooperation is not only a tool for supplementing financial resources but also for promoting the mayor's political legitimacy and influence in the local community and the national political arena. As devolution progressed through decentralization, mayors increased their political influence even in national elections (legislative and presidential). The political influence of the mayor might have helped his promotion in his political party, *Renaissance du Bénin*, the dominant party during the Soglo administration (1991–96). Glèlè-Ahanhanzo ascended to his current status in his party, being appointed as the fourth vice president from his former post as the director of the youth section. He was also the president of the National Mayors' Association, the ANCB. He was later appointed as the Minister of Environment under the second (final) administration of President Yayi. We can perceive that the case of Glèlè-Ahanhanzo is one of the most outstanding cases in terms of the political impact of decentralization in Africa (Iwata 2012a, 156–57).

3.5. Political Turbulence in Decentralizing Local Governance

3.5.1. Politicizing Local Governance

While African countries began to tackle decentralization because of the (*de facto*) conditionality for receiving foreign aid, Western donor countries naïvely expected that decentralization would foster "local" democracy in Africa. Rather, decentralization made local governance more politicized instead of straightforwardly bringing about socio-economic development and local democracy in the short term, especially in politically liberalizing countries, such as Benin since the beginning of the 1990s and Burkina Faso after the Compaoré regime ended in 2014.

Following the Beninese cases, we can see similar ongoing phenomena in local politics in Burkina Faso after the regime turnover in 2014. It might be an important lesson for reflecting on the relationship between decentralization and local democracy. Contrary to the naïve idea in earlier years that decentralization brings about local democracy, it significantly stimulates local politics in a nonlinear way with the progress of democratization.

In addition to the over-politicization of local governance, decentralization obviously expanded the gap between urban and rural local governments through the acceleration of international cooperation among local governments (Iwata 2012a, 158).

It seems that rapid urbanization accelerated the politicization of local governance. As the city became bigger, the requests from people to the local government and its leaders were amplified and increasingly diversified. Local politicians themselves work in their own interests in local politics. In the Beninese local government system, councilors of the commune have a "voluntary" status, receiving no regular salary for their services, although this does not mean that they cannot access certain financial remunerations or budget for the commune's management. This scenario made it more likely that local councilors would seek personal and political goals using their political status and influence. Urbanization increasingly made local politics more dynamic in African countries in light of the increasing populations, mandates, and budgets of local governments and their leaders.

Therefore, the election of a mayor and appointments to other important posts after a municipal election would likely heat up the Commune Council (Congress) politically. When the Commune Council becomes a battlefield among personal interests for political parties' power struggles, making it easy to forget the promises made during an electoral campaign, the local government becomes unmanageable and cannot make any decisions regarding the development projects of the commune unless a certain political party occupies the majority of the Commune Council. Consequently, local residents lose their confidence and criticize their local representatives.

After the first municipal election in 2003, since decentralization started, Benin held the following local elections in 2008, 2015, and 2020. After each election, the political instability and over-politicization brought about serious stagnations in commune governance. The most remarkable case is the motion of discharge against the mayor brought by councilors in the Commune Council, mobilizing a vote of nonconfidence (*défiance*). A storm of discharge of mayors came again in Benin within one year after the latest municipal election.

Even after the first and second local elections, the Commune Council continued to be a political battlefield in the rivalry between political parties and local politicians (Dangnon 2009, 95). Local governance was politicized for political, personal, and financial interests (Dangnon 2009, 89, 101), while services for the development and management of the local community were neglected. Thus, the situation dissatisfied local residents and voters, who perceived the local politicians as immersing themselves in political games for their own ends (Dangnon 2009, 103). The moment of the election of the mayor made local governance exciting and highly politicized. The political battle for ruling the commune divided the political parties represented in the Commune Council (Dangnon 2009, 92). When a certain party does not comfortably dominate the Commune Council, commune management is unlikely to run smoothly. In the worst case, the mayor can be discharged by their own council through nonconfidence voting.

Finally, to tranquilize the over-politicization of commune governance, the Commission for Decentralization, the supervising organization of decentralization, warned the communes that the Commune Council is not a battlefield for seeking individual political interests (Dangnon 2009, 89). Despite repeated calls and interventions of the Commission for Decentralization, political disputes and storms of discharge trials against mayors continued (Dangnon 2009, 90–91). However, discharging a mayor did not necessarily make commune governance peaceful; in fact, such actions often invited second discharge motions.

The discharge of mayors has not only been caused by the struggles among local political actors but also brought about due to political battles at the national level, especially between the president (and his leading party) and the opposition (Dangnon 2009, 95). Under the current rule, the mayor can be discharged relatively easily by collecting two-thirds of the commune councilors' nonconfidence votes. This system might be reconsidered in order to make local governance more stable and functional (Dangnon 2009, 150).

In addition to the politicization of local governance, local governments face serious challenges of administrative incapacity (Dangnon 2009, 152–53). In the decentralization process, the devolution of human resources is stipulated by the central government to the communes. However, the devolution of human resources has not occurred in a comparable manner to that of financial resources. This administrative incapacity has allowed local politicians to exhibit more politicized behaviors.

3.5.2. Storms of Discharge of Mayors after Local Elections

The councilors of the commune are directly elected by voters in their local constituency in a proportional electoral system according to the list of candidates submitted by political parties or groups. Then, the elected councilors of the commune elect the mayor (currently serving as the chairman of the Commune Council).[16]

In Benin and Burkina Faso, the Commune Council (assembly) is able to discharge its mayor relatively easily by collecting two-thirds of the nonconfidence vote among the commune councilors, according to the decentralization-related law (Iwata 2012a, 152).[17] Under the current system, it is possible for the discharge of the mayor to occur after the regime change of the central government directly affects the political power balance in the Commune Council. For local residents, it is not possible to intervene in such political disputes among politicians after a local election is held (Hassani 2016).

When the mayoral race is launched, local politicians inevitably begin to immerse themselves in the political game while pursuing their personal and political interests instead of seriously working for the development of the commune. Thus, local residents will be dissatisfied with the performances of the mayor and Commune Council.

---

[16] Law N° 2013-06 on the Electoral Code in the Republic of Benin, in its article 400 paragraph 2, provides that "the candidate for mayor is proposed by the list obtaining the absolute majority of the commune councilors" (Hassani 2016).

[17] Article 53 of Law N° 97-029 of January 15, 1999, on the organization of municipalities in the Republic of Benin and its implementing Decree N° 2005-376 of June 23, 2005, fixing the terms of dismissal of the Mayor (Hassani 2016). Art 275 of Law N° 055-2004 / AN on the general code of the local governments in Burkina Faso.

This part generally examines cases in Benin because Burkina Faso has not sufficiently experienced local governance and decentralization yet under the democratic political circumstance for reflecting on the political impact of decentralization. In general, the political impact of decentralization should be more prominent in democratizing regimes rather than in authoritarian regimes. Benin began confronting the challenge of democratization in 1990. On the contrary, Burkina Faso only started the democratization process in 2014, after former President Compaoré was ousted by the insurgency.

3.5.2.1. Cases in Benin

The third municipal elections in Benin took place in 2015 (Boko 2015; Le blog de la présse béninoise 2015). Municipal elections should be held every five years according to the decentralization-related law. This second election had to take place in 2013. It was delayed by two years due to political, technical, and financial reasons.

In the election of 2015, the President Yayi-supporting party *Forces cauris pour un Bénin émergent* (FCBE, Cowrie Forces for an Emerging Benin) could not sustain a dominant force in the Commune Council, although it retained a minimal influence in the northern regions (Boko 2015).

One year after that municipal election, mayors were once again discharged, causing political turbulence and confusion in the Beninese communes. After the election of President Talon in March 2016, at least seven mayors (including major communes, such as Parakou and Djougou) were discharged by the Commune Council in the second half of 2016. In addition, many cases of discharge are still in progress in Commune Councils (Hassani 2016).

It was not the first political storm involving the discharge of mayors during the last two decades of decentralization and democratization in Benin. Such an incident had already happened after the first and second municipal elections held in 2003 and 2008, respectively. We can recognize this situation as an institutional problem of local governance in Benin. Publicly, the reason for the discharge of mayors was announced by Commune Councils as the "bad (too arbitrary) management" of the mayor (Africa No.1 2016).

However, these incidents, in addition to political disputes in local governments, also seem to have been politically orchestrated by the state authority. This storm of discharges started again after the latest presidential election took place in 2016. The election of President Talon, a millionaire businessman who unexpectedly defeated the "promised" candidate Zinsou, son of the former President of the Republic and backed by almost all "established" political leaders and their political parties, surprised Benin and the world.

The municipal elections took place in June 2015, the final year of the Yayi administration. President Yayi was elected in 2006 for the first time and re-elected in 2011 and would end his final (second) five-year presidential term (stipulated by the Constitution of Benin) in 2016. The discharged mayors belonged to the supporting party for the former president (FCBE). They were elected by the majority of the Commune Councils thanks to the influence of then-President Yayi.

After President Yayi left the presidential office in April 2016, some mayors lost their strong political backing to continue behaving as the local "big man" and were recognized as political opponents by the newly elected President Talon (Bénin Web TV 2016; Slm 2016). Seemingly, the regime change in national politics significantly affected local politics.

In reality, the Support Fund for the Development of Communes (*Fonds d'appui au développement des communes*, FADEC)[18] expressed its concern about the severe, irregular acts and breaches in 30 communes among the 77 communes in Benin, for which there were no punishments. In addition, FADEC also revealed the absence of a financial report related to international cooperation with foreign partners (Hassani 2016).

In October 2016, the ANCB urgently called for the councilors of communes to end their political disputes and requested the discharge of the mayor whom they had elected to normalize local politics in Benin (Africa No.1 2016; Benin Medias 2016).

Despite the wave of discharges, some mayors were able to retain their position, such as Mayor Adjovi of Ouidah, the heart of tourism and vodun (traditional religious practices, also known as voodoo) in Benin. He was accused of arbitrary commune management, and the commune councilors requested a special meeting on his discharge. Finally, the nonconfidence vote was held in February 2017, collecting 12 votes for discharge among 19 councilors (only one vote below the required number to discharge the mayor). According to the "two-thirds rule," Adjovi barely escaped discharge by just one vote. However, his political influence was definitely damaged in his commune, as the majority of councilors had attempted to oust him (Meton 2017).

The storm of discharge of mayors finally reached the commune of Abomey. As mentioned earlier, Abomey is governed by Mayor Glèlè-Ahanhanzo, one of the most prominent political actors in the decentralization process of Benin, which revived tradition in its modern political system. However, he was not safe

---

[18] This is a governmental organization established in 2008 under the Ministry of Decentralization and Local Governance to support the financial devolution from the central government to local governments (communes).

from this politicized storm. He also faced a discharge motion attempt from the group of councilors of Abomey commune because of his arbitrary nomination of vice mayors and suspicious management of the public market (Gbaguidi 2016). The issue of public market management has always brought about the biggest disputes between the central government and local governments in the decentralization process in Benin because it is a question related to financial resources, which directly affects political interests.

This storm of discharges of mayors seems to have expanded after the regime change brought about by Mr. Talon's election as President of the Republic. Mayors who were discharged or are in the process of being discharged generally belong to the political parties that supported Zinsou in the presidential election held in March 2016. After the presidential election, dominant parties in the Yayi administration became the opposition against the new president. President Talon was a businessman and participated in the election as an independent (anti-establishment) candidate. Whether the president's will influences or not, the political storm in local governments is significantly intertwined with national politics. For President Talon, the determined reformer, it was favorable to reduce the opposition's influence in local government to carry out his draconian policy throughout the country.

However, there was predictable political pressure because Mayor Glèlè-Ahanhanzo supported Zinsou, the candidate opposing the "establishment" camp, and thus the current President Talon, during the presidential election campaign according to the decision of his party, *Renaissance du Benin* (Benin Web TV). Although Glèlè-Ahanhanzo does not belong to FCBE, the party that supported former President Yayi, he has a greater reason to be personally targeted by President Talon, as he was the Minister of Environment in the former Yayi administration.

Seemingly, President Talon tried to discharge Glèlè-Ahanhanzo because he (his party) had supported Zinsou in the last presidential election while accusing Glèlè-Ahanhanzo of bad usage of commune resources (e.g., purchase of vehicles and foreign trips). However, this time, the opponent councilors of the Abomey Commune Council could not carry out nonconfidence voting. His prestigious origin, deriving from the former Dahomey Kingdom, might have saved him from discharge. The serious division among councilors in the Commune Council of Abomey remains since the unsuccessful trial for discharge. Thus, Mr. Glèlè-Ahanhanzo has had to behave more carefully in conducting his policies since this incident. Although President Talon could not remove Glèlè-Ahanhanzo, he could significantly damage his influence on local politics in Abomey.

This tug-of-war between the president and opposition mayors finally reached Cotonou, the economic capital of Benin. Since the beginning of the decentralization process, Cotonou has been governed by the Soglo family. The first mayor after decentralization started, Nicéphore Soglo, was the former president of the Republic of Benin (1991–96). President Soglo's party, *Renaissance du Benin*, has led Benin as the ruling party or has been the influential opposition party since democratization started in Benin in 1990. After a decade of his governance of Cotonou, his son, Léhady Soglo, was elected Mayor of Cotonou in 2015. As in the case of Abomey, *Renaissance du Benin* is one of the biggest opponents of the current President Talon, who strongly supported Zinsou in the last presidential election of 2016.

The Talon administration increased its pressure on the Cotonou commune's governance, ordering the governor of Littoral prefecture (the supervising administrative body over Cotonou commune) to deploy radical measures for local management, such as clean-up campaigns in public spaces of the city aimed at removing informal small businesses from the roadside, which often create heavy traffic jams, and arresting traders of fake medicine. Such draconian measures have been considered "necessary" and appropriate for economic development and public health, but dangerous for the mayor and "establishment" politicians with regard to their popularity and re-election.

In July 2017, the central government finally dismissed the Mayor of Cotonou, Léhady Soglo, due to "heavy errors" and bad management (e.g., arbitrary sale of national assets, violations of administrative ethics, and arbitrary financial measures for giving himself a bonus). The Minister of Decentralization signed this order. When a mayor is suspended, the first vice mayor temporarily succeeds in this function (Ague 2017).

3.5.2.2. Cases in Burkina Faso

Compared to Benin, Burkina Faso is still less experienced in terms of democratically organized elections, although local elections were repeatedly held under the authoritarian regime, before President Compaoré resigned in 2014. Time is required to sufficiently examine how decentralization affects the local politics in Burkina Faso. However, there have been some signs of change in local governance in Burkina Faso since this regime turnover occurred.

Under the 27 years of Compaoré's authoritarian rule, Burkina Faso was known as the model of decentralization. The dominant party, *le Congrès pour la démocratie et le progrès* (CDP, the Congress for Democracy and Progress), founded to support President Compaoré, dominated all political institutions, including the local government under his regime. Accordingly, there were a few places where local politics heated up under the Compaoré administration. Therefore, the municipal elections held in 2016—three decades after the revolutionary and authoritarian regimes established in the 1980s—were the first democratically organized local elections for the Burkinabe people.

After the organization of local elections, the same kind of political confusion that existed in Benin was present in the Burkinabe local governments. The selection of the mayor and other important posts in the communes created a serious stagnation of local governance, as the paralyzed Commune Councils, which lacked dominant political forces, could not make decisions. In the local election held in May 2016, the new dominant party, *le Mouvement pour le peuple et progrès* (MPP, the Movement for People and Progress),[19] could not win local elections to ensure its comfortable situation in local governments compared to the presidential and legislative elections that took place in November 2015 (Journal du Jeudi 2016).

In December 2016, Mayor Zongo (Boulmiougou ward in Ouagadougou) was discharged by the Commune Council for his arbitrary management, collecting ten nonconfidence votes among 13 councilors.[20] After this decision, his furious supporters burned down and destroyed the ward-city hall (Nabole December 7; December 10, 2016). Since the first local election took place after Compaoré stepped down, local governance in Burkina Faso has been involved in a political storm as the baptism of democratization.

In the Sapone Commune Council, councilors were bitterly divided into two groups at the moment of the selection of mayor. The commune councilors were barely able to select an MPP candidate. However, the mayor was unable to even call the commune council because of the opposition's boycott.

In the Banfora Commune Council, the worst situation occurred. Although the new dominant party, MPP, ensured a comfortable number of seats in the Commune Council after the local election, the party was divided because it had two different candidates. After repeated disputes and negotiations, the mayor was selected from the minor party. Finally, the central government announced the cancellation of the election and re-election for 19 communes in May 2017

---

[19] The most important aides, such as Salifou Diallo, Roch Christian Kabore, and Simon Compaoré, left CDP and then established their new opposition party (*le Mouvement du peuple pour le progrès*, MPP) in January 2014 against President Compaoré. During the last presidential election of 2010, Compaoré promised them that he would not remain in power after his "last" term. However, he tried to modify the Constitution to secure himself as "president for life." These close collaborators were disappointed by Compaoré's violation of his promise and abandoned him (Interview with MPP member, August 20, 2014, Ouagadougou).

[20] Art 275 of Law N° 055-2004 / AN on the general code of the local governments in Burkina Faso.

to restart local governance (Burkina 24, March 1, May 31, 2017; Nabole, May 29, 2017).

In Benin, the selection of mayor and other important posts in a Commune Council has occasionally led to serious disputes as well as stagnation in local governance in certain communes that are not comfortably composed of members of the dominant party. However, the situation is more complex in Burkina Faso because it has simultaneously tackled significant political reforms of democratization and decentralization. This is a significant difference from Benin, which initiated democratization before decentralization.

3.6. Conclusion

This chapter tackled the question of the political impact of decentralization in urbanizing African countries. First, this chapter revisited the history of decentralization in Africa. Then, it examined the effects of decentralization on African politics and international relations through case studies of Benin and Burkina Faso, such as local elections, decentralized cooperation, and post-electoral political disputes in local governments.

On the one hand, decentralization has been gradually but steadily changing the political landscape from the local to national, then international levels in Africa, although it was not a panacea-like institutional reform as the Western donor countries and international organizations had expected earlier. On the other hand, decentralization obviously reduced the distance between African local governments and the globalizing world (Iwata 2012a, 159).

Decentralization significantly diversified and transformed the world of the "political imaginary" (Banégas 2003, 153), which has created political momentum in African countries. Decentralization has the potential to redraw political boundaries between local governments, the national government, and the international community. Insofar as decentralization keeps progressing, local politics will more directly affect the politics in the national arena, such as questions about democratization. Local political actors, such as mayors and commune councilors, need more attention in the study of African politics. Local governments significantly entered into the arena of international cooperation and diplomacy through decentralized cooperation in an extraversive approach. It is no longer sufficient to examine the political process conducted only in capital cities to understand the political transformation in African countries that have experienced full-scale decentralization (Iwata 2012a, 160).

The progress of democratization also enhances the political impact of decentralization. The simultaneous operation of democratization and decentralization might bring about more complicated challenges in African politics. It is not easy to examine the correlation between democratization and decentralization in African countries using a simplistic framework. However, it might be favorable to begin the process of decentralization after consolidating the democratization process for African countries to mitigate political shock, confusion, and violence in the process of enacting political and administrative reforms (Iwata 2011, 109).

Chapter 4

Borders in Africa's International Relations: Reflection on the Borders of the French Colony *Upper Volta*[1]

It came into being in 1919 but was then abolished in 1932 and again reconstituted by a law of 4 September 1947, which stated that the boundaries of "the re-established territory of Upper Volta" were to be "those of the former colony of Upper Volta on 5 September 1932,"... In the present case, therefore, the problem is to ascertain what frontier was inherited from the French administration; more precisely, to ascertain what, in the disputed area, was the frontier that existed in 1959–1960 between the *territoires d'outre-mer* of Sudan[2] and Upper Volta. (ICJ 1986c, 6)

4.1 Introduction

This chapter is intended to examine the origin of border (political and geographical boundary) issues that have raised concerns and caused discord in African politics and international relations since the independence of African countries.

The final border beacon (*la borne* in French) for territorial delimitation between Burkina Faso (former Upper Volta) and Mali was established in 2010. An inaugural ceremony took place among representatives of both governments. After long, tough negotiations involving the Organisation of African Unity (OAU, founded in 1963 and reformed into the African Union [AU] in 2002), the Economic Community of West African States (ECOWAS), and especially accepting the judgment of the International Court of Justice (ICJ), both countries eventually agreed on the delimitation of their border. Thus, the border disputes between the governments of Burkina Faso and Mali were peacefully resolved 50 years after both countries attained independence.

---

[1] This chapter was originally published in the journal of the International Studies Association of Ritsumeikan University (Kyoto, Japan): Iwata, T. (2021). Revisiting Border Issues in Africa: a reflection on the border of the French colony Upper Volta. *Ritsumeikan Annual Review of International Studies, 20*, 1–23.

[2] French Sudan colony, currently Mali.

Burkina Faso and Mali had fought two wars over the border—the first in 1974 and the second in 1985. In the 1974 war, the name of a young soldier, future revolutionary leader Thomas Sankara, was spread widely in Upper Volta (the name Burkina Faso was adopted in 1984) in narrating how bravely he had fought to enter Malian territory (Jaffré 1997, 92). This war made Sankara famous among the Voltaic people (the people of Upper Volta have been called Burkinabe since 1984). This war provided young military leaders with an opportunity to join in the political game and finally establish their revolutionary regime (1983–87) in Upper Volta (Burkina Faso), led by Sankara with Compaoré[3] and other young comrades.

The independence of African countries generated political and diplomatic disputes domestically and internationally over sovereign borders, as newly sovereign African states retained their colonial borders. Although territorial borders had been delimited or imposed by European empires to rule their colonies, African countries were unable to show more "authentic" borders as a more legitimate alternative. Thus, the OAU recognized the principle of respect for the current (inherited) borders in 1964.[4]

The AU subsequently inherited the principle of maintaining the status quo of national borders from the OAU. Under this principle, African states have tried to resolve domestic and international disputes derived from border problems. Since independence, international border disputes have rarely brought about inter-state wars between African national armies. However, internally, many African states have faced rebel struggles, such as separatist movements in Katanga (DR Congo), Cabinda (Angola), and Casamance (Senegal) or those seeking the reunification of compatriot groups divided by the imposition of colonial borders, such as the Great Somali movement (spreading over Somalia, Djibouti, Ethiopia, and Kenya) and Ewe unification movement (Ghana and Togo). Eritrea (1993) and South Sudan (2011) achieved independence after long and painful armed struggles.

After a referendum in January 2011, South Sudan gained independence from Sudan in July of that year. This most recent independence event in Africa was recognized by the international community. However, South Sudan's independence has also been considered Pandora's box. This modification of the border encouraged separatist movements from which many African

---

[3] After 27 years of authoritarian rule, Compaoré resigned at the end of October 2014 after the immensely popular insurgency caused by a protest movement against his attempt at a constitutional change to remove presidential term limits.

[4] The OAU's 1964 resolution (AHG/16/1) determined incumbent national borders among African countries. The OAU charter recognized respect for the actual sovereignty and territory of African countries (Touval 1972, 42, 86).

countries have suffered. From this perspective, South Sudan's independence is not simply a domestic issue in a specific country but might affect the destinies of all African states.

In general, armed conflicts or civil wars occur once inside a country and occasionally expand to neighboring countries, but cases of inter-state war between African states' national armies derived from border disputes, such as the Uganda–Tanzania war in 1978–79, have been rare. In addition, the two wars (in 1974 and 1985) between the national armies of Burkina Faso (Upper Volta) and Mali, due to their border disputes, are not recognized as typically armed conflicts in postcolonial African history.

This chapter revisits the origin of border issues, which have threatened national and regional security in African countries, by focusing on the French colony of Upper Volta as a case study. Newly independent African countries had to inherit their colonial borders and territories. However, the situation has been more complicated for Upper Volta (Burkina Faso) because it was first established as a French colonial administrative unit (*circonscription administrative*) under *Afrique occidentale française* (AOF, French West Africa) in 1919, then was abolished in 1932, was reestablished in 1947, and subsequently achieved independence in 1960. At the time when this colony unit was reestablished, some parts of the colonial administrative borders were vague and remained so until the day of independence. This unelaborate transition of the colonial administrative unit in the French colony made the border issue of Upper Volta (Burkina Faso) more complicated and controversial with neighboring countries after its independence.

Although this chapter neither concludes nor generalizes Africa's border issues through these case studies, it contributes some essential understandings of the border-originated challenges among African countries.

4.2. Colonial and Contemporary Border Disputes in Africa

Globalization is perceived as a fundamental feature of the contemporary world. People, capital, information, and infectious diseases have been crossing sovereign borders rapidly and in large quantities. Although globalization has progressed, sovereign borders never disappear and sustain their significant influence over people's lives. The COVID-19 pandemic has mercilessly locked us within sovereign borders.

Borders are likely to create "outsiders," and not only in the geographical sense. Borders have influenced and edified communities' and individuals' identities and have constituted the base of political conflict. The demarcation of borders is part of the sovereign state formation process. However, European countries drew extremely artificial borders in Africa after the Berlin Conference

(1884–85) without respecting the interests and histories of (political) communities of African people.

Colonial borders became sovereign, international borders among African states on their first day of independence. Thus, the border issue is old but constantly renewed for African states even six decades after their independence. Borders have affected territorial disputes, armed conflicts, national security, refugee issues, regional integration, sovereignty, smuggling, and trade disputes. However, newly independent African states have maintained the status quo and have been reluctant to discuss border modifications.

Even in the absence of physical conflict (though not necessarily during peaceful periods), the border issue is always very sensitive in relation to the activities of anti-government rebel forces or smugglers.

The African states have recognized that modifying state borders might open Pandora's box and lead to their fragmentation (Touval 1972, 83). In the early 1960s, the demand for Eritrea's independence from Ethiopia divided African countries into two camps: the Casablanca Group and the Monrovia Group. The OAU called on African countries to respect the "inherited" borders from former European countries.

Sovereign borders had existed among African states in precolonial times as well. The continent has a long history of numerous kingdoms and chieftaincies being established and perishing with accompanying border modifications. However, the governing authorities did not necessarily draw hard geographical borders. Consequently, the rule in a peripheral region would become ambiguous in the traditional African states. In African history, massive numbers of people or ethnic groups repeatedly crossed sovereign borders, for example, to escape tyranny (Herbst 2000, 88).

Two categories can be distinguished in terms of the approach to delimiting colonial borders. The first category includes borders rectified by agreements among European colonial forces. Thus, the borders were international borders between European colonies. The second category includes borders rectified inside a colony (Touval 1972, 4). In other words, colonies contained domestic and administrative borders. These colonial borders divided ethnic groups and living areas and created new identities and interests among African people (Nugent 2002, 273).

4.3. Origin of Border Issues in Upper Volta (Burkina Faso)

4.3.1. Establishment and Reformation of Upper Volta

Despite repeated contestations and dissatisfaction with the colonial borders, newly independent African states had to inherit these borders because they could not present more legitimate sovereign borders. Upper Volta (Burkina Faso since 1984) experienced this typical process, but its border circumstances were more complicated than those of other African countries because of its particular colonial experience.

The Upper Volta colony was established in 1919, then abolished in 1932, and eventually reestablished in 1947 by the French government. During its abolition period, the former Upper Volta territory was divided into three parts. These territories were then absorbed into three different neighboring French colonies by 1947: Côte d'Ivoire, French Sudan (*Soudan français*, currently Mali), and Niger. Thus, the border situation of Upper Volta complicated its relationships with neighboring countries just after the country attained independence.

After the conquest against African chieftaincies' resistance, in 1895, the French colonial authority established the AOF comprising Senegal, Côte d'Ivoire, Guinea, and French Sudan. The AOF was then restructured by adding Dahomey, Upper Volta, Mauritania, and Niger.

The AOF tried to establish its administrative structure and fix the colonial administrative borders of Upper Volta with neighboring colonies.[5] However, at the beginning of the twentieth century, the colonial administrative unit and the AOF's borders were frequently modified. For instance, the Tera region was transferred from the Upper Volta colony to the Niger colony in 1927.[6]

The Fada N'Gourma region (southeastern part of Upper Volta) was transferred from the Dahomey colony to the Senegal-Niger colony before the Upper Volta

---

[5] A report on northern Upper Volta laid out the modification of military territory borders and establishment of the Bandiagara, Sumpi, and Ouahigouya cercles. Gouvernement général de l'Afrique Occidentale Française, "Le délégué permanant du Gouverneur Général à Monsieur le Gouverneur Général de l'Afrique Occidentale Française" [General government of the AOF, "The permanent delegate of the Governor-General to Mr. Governor-General of French West Africa"], Saint-Louis, December 26, 1902. Archives nationales d'outre-mer [National Overseas Archives, ANOM], Aix-en-Provence, France. A report on villages located across the border between the Dori and Fada cercles. Le Gouverneur Général de l'Afrique Occidentale Française au Ministre des Colonies, "Rectification de frontière entre les résidences du Dori (1er territoire militaire) et de Fada N'Gourma (Dahomey)" [The Governor-General of French West Africa to the Minister of Colonies, "Rectification of the border between the residences of Dori <1st military territory> and Fada N'Gourma <Dahomey>"], Saint Louis, August 7, 1901. ANOM.

[6] Lettre confidentiale au inspecteur général des colonies [Confidential letter to the inspector general of the colonies], January 23, 1947. (Centre national des archives du Burkina Faso [National Center of Archives of Burkina Faso, CNA-BF])

colony was established.[7] The AOF reported to the French metropolitan government that the Fada *cercle* (similar to a prefectural administrative structure) and a part of the Kandi cercle were transferred from the Dahomey colony to the Senegal-Niger colony. This was because the people of Fada N'Gourma were a closer ethnic group to the Mossi and did not have a common culture with the Baliba people of Dahomey. Rivers did not necessarily separate the inhabited territories of ethnic groups clearly; the same ethnic groups usually lived on both sides of the river. A report presented that the French colonial authority tried to focus on categorizing indigenous peoples' living areas rather than distinguishing geographical landmarks.[8]

The government ordinance of March 2, 1907, modified the borders between the two colonies.[9] The AOF indicated the necessity of considering people living in the inter-colony border area. The presidential ordinance officialized this decision. However, this modification of borders and territories remained ambiguous in the colonial territories and repeatedly caused border disputes between Dahomey (Benin) and Upper Volta (Burkina Faso) after their independence.

The colonial government recognized the Gourmantché as a neighboring ethnic group of the Mossi people, although they did not belong to the same ethnic group or the same political community. A colonial officer reported that the chief of Bilanga had to belong to the N'Gourma cercle for fixing the Mossi and Ngourmas resident regions because the chief of Bilanga was under the King of Gourma's influence.[10]

---

[7] "Décret portant modification de la limite du Haut-Sénégal-Niger et du Dahomey" ["Decree of the modification of the boundary of Haut-Senegal-Niger and Dahomey"], April 23, 1913. ANOM. "Rapport au Président de la république française suivi d'un décret portant modification de la limite du Haut-Sénégal-Niger et du Dahomey" ["Report to the President of the French Republic followed by a decree modifying the boundary of Haut-Senegal-Niger and Dahomey"], April 23, 1913. ANOM.

[8] Gouvernement Général de l'Afrique Occidentale Française, "Rapport en conseil de gouvernement" [General Government of French West Africa, "Report to the Council of Government"], December 13, 1906. ANOM.

[9] "Décret portant modification de la limite du Haut-Sénégal-Niger et du Dahomey" ["Decree modifying the boundary of Haut-Senegal-Niger and Dahomey"], April 23, 1907. ANOM.

[10] Soudan Français, "Projet de la délimitation des territoires de la Boucle du Niger entre les colonies du Dahomey et du Soudan Français" [French Sudan, "Project for the delimitation of the territories of the Niger loop between the colonies of Dahomey and French Sudan"], September 8, 1898. ANOM.

Figure 4.1. Colonial border between the Dahomey and French Sudan colonies
under the AOF

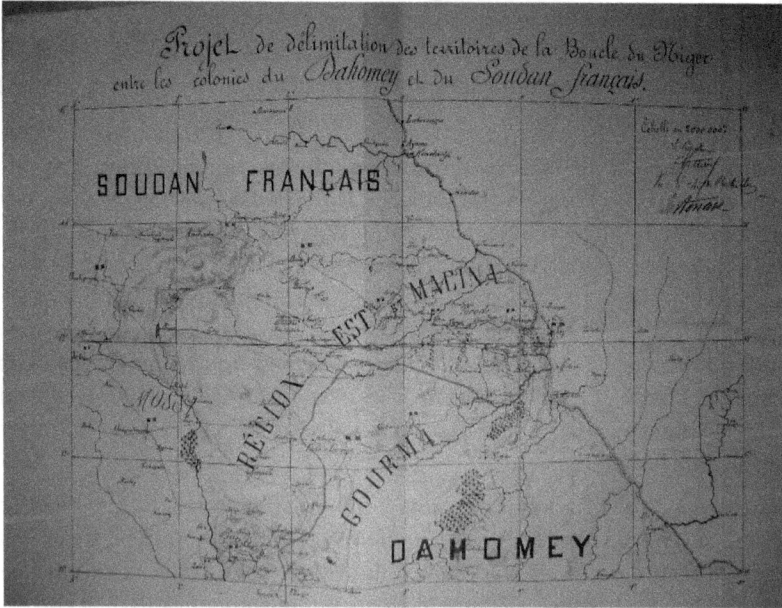

Source: Première direction, Bureau de l'Afrique, "Soudan Française: Projet de
délimitation des territoires de la Boucle du Niger entre les colonies du Dahomey et du
Soudan Français" [First Direction, Africa Office, "French Sudan: Project of Delimitation
of the Territories of the Niger Loop between the Colonies of Dahomey and French
Sudan"], September 16, 1898. ANOM.

The Upper Volta colony in the AOF was established in 1919 under suspicion
regarding the economic gain for France from this new colony. After its
establishment, its cercle units were reviewed. Within the next ten years, many
of these cercles were restructured and de facto downgraded into subdivisions
(lower administrative units). Certain subdivisions were subsequently abolished.
For example, the Leo subdivision was abolished and transferred under the Pô
subdivision.[11] The Yako subdivision was abolished and transferred under the
Koudougou subdivision.[12] The Diapaga subdivision was removed and transferred
under the Fada cercle. The most crucial measure was the abolition of the

---

[11] "Arreté No. 53," Administrateur en chef des colonies lieutenant-gouverneur P.I. de
Haute-Volta ["Ordinance No. 53," Chief Colonial Administrator P.I. Lieutenant-Governor
of Upper Volta], March 20, 1929. CNA-BF.

[12] "Arreté No. 70", Administrateur en chef des colonies lieutenant-gouverneur P.I. de
Haute-Volta ["Ordinance No. 70," Chief Colonial Administrator P.I. Lieutenant-Governor
of Upper Volta], April 6, 1929. CNA-BF.

military post in the Bobo-Dioulasso cercle in 1929.[13] The AOF downgraded Upper Volta's position in the colonial structure and then prepared to abolish the colony a decade after its establishment.

4.3.2. Abolition and Reestablishment of Upper Volta

Thus, the Upper Volta colony was first abolished by the presidential ordinance (*Décret*) of September 1932. Its territory was divided and absorbed into three neighboring AOF colonies.[14] The Fada and Dori cercles (268,000 persons) were transferred to the Niger colony. The Ouahigouya cercle and regions on the Volta River's left side (a part of the Dedougou cercle; 712,000 persons) were transferred to the French Sudan colony. The most populated and more crucial regions of Upper Volta, such as the Batié, Bobo-Dioulasso, Gaoua, Kaya, Koudougou, Ouagadougou, and Tenkodogo cercles and another part of the Dedougou cercle (2,019,000 persons), were transferred to the Côte d'Ivoire colony (Skinner 1964, 173) and then reclassified as the sub-region of northern Côte d'Ivoire in July 1937.

After Upper Volta's abolition, colonial administrative institutions, like the military and postal headquarters, were removed from the former Upper Volta colony.[15] According to an AOF report, the Upper Volta colony had not been economically profitable for France since its establishment in 1919.[16] The AOF governor's report addressing the Minister of Colony recommended reforming

---

[13] Gouverneur général de l'AOF. "Arreté Portant la suppression du poste militaire définitif de Hound (cercle de Bobo-Dioulasso)" [Governor-General of the AOF, "Ordinance relating the abolition of the final military post of Hound, Cercle of Bobo-Dioulasso"], April 18, 1929. CNA-BF.

[14] Décret du 5 septembre 1932, "Portant suppression de la colonie de la Haute-Volta et répartition entre les colonies du Niger, du Soudan et de la Côte d'Ivoire" [Decree of September 5, 1932, "Relating the abolition of the colony of the Upper Volta and distributing it among the colonies of Niger, Sudan and Côte d'Ivoire"]. ANOM.

[15] Le Gouvernment général de l'AOF, "Note pour le directeur général des services économiques" [The General Government of the AOF, "Note for the Director General of Economic Services"], September 24, 1932. CNA-BF.

[16] Lettre du Lieutenant-Gouverneur de la Côte d'Ivoire au Gouverneur Général, "Rémaniements térritoriaux Haute Volta," [Letter from the Lieutenant-Governor of Côte d'Ivoire to the Governor General, "Territorial Changes of Upper Volta"], April 19, 1932. CNA-BF.

the AOF structure by abolishing Upper Volta. At that time, the Mauritania colony became economically more attractive than Upper Volta to France.[17]

The Governor of the Côte d'Ivoire colony reported to the Governor-General of the AOF (located in Dakar) that the cost of keeping the Upper Volta colony was "unreasonably expensive" for the French government given its small economic benefits and recommended its abolition as a realistic reform in April 1932. The Chamber of Commerce of the AOF reported in June 1932 that it would not face any problems with Upper Volta's abolition. An economic division reported that Ouahigouya and the northern part were transferred to French Sudan because of pasturage activities. The French media also reported that Upper Volta had contributed little to the colonial economy.[18] Thus, the Upper Volta colony's establishment was due to more political reasons than economic profitability. Its reestablishment 15 years after its abolition continued to raise political issues even after its independence.

The abolition period of the Upper Volta colony (1932–47) was significant in that it saw delayed infrastructure development in the territory. Given this situation, the Voltaic people, especially traditional Mossi chiefs, were greatly concerned about decreasing their presence in the French colony. Consequently, after World War II, Mossi chiefs, especially the supreme Mossi chief Moro Naba (of Ouagadougou), strengthened the requirements placed on the colonial government for reestablishing Upper Volta.[19]

In particular, Moro Naba claimed that a modification of electoral law would reduce his region's political power. Furthermore, the railway construction project at Bobo-Dioulasso (from Abidjan) had been suspended for over ten years. The colonial government's promise to extend the railway to Ouagadougou had yet to be carried out. Moro Naba understood that this delay was due to the abolition of the Upper Volta colony, which downgraded its status in the colonial structure. Moro Naba established the *Union Voltaïque* (Voltaic Union) in March 1946, calling on the French government to reestablish the Upper Volta colony by separating it from northern Côte d'Ivoire. The Voltaic Union elected Moro Naba as the honorable president.[20]

---

[17] Le gouverneur général de l'AOF à Monsieur le Ministre des Colonies, "Réorganisation territorial des colonies de l'AOF" [From the Governor-General of the AOF to Minister of Colonies, "Territorial Reorganization of colonies of the AOF"], April 7, 1932. CNA-BF.

[18] *1er Nouvelle*, June 28, 1932. CNA-BF.

[19] Letter from Moro-Naba, Emperor of Mossi, to M.G. Bidault Président de council (September 4, 1946, Ouagadougou). CNA-BF.

[20] Lettre confidentiale de l'administrateur des colonies au directeur général des affaires politiques, administratives et sociales de l'AOF [Confidential letter from the administrator of

At this moment, France worried that Moro Naba would approach the British colonial authority owing to his dissatisfaction with the abolition of the Upper Volta colony. Indeed, Moro Naba did receive a British delegation. Consequently, the AOF reported concern about Moro Naba's sympathy for the British colonial administration.[21]

France also worried about the increasing power of Ivoirian political leaders, especially Félix Houphouët-Boigny, and began to consider reestablishing Upper Volta to reduce his influence in the French colony (Skinner 1964, 183). However, France did not find a particular economic interest in upgrading Upper Volta to a colony again. In fact, France expected that it would cost (financial and human resources) more if the Upper Volta colony was reestablished. The sole interest of France was to supply labor sources from the (former) Upper Volta territory to the AOF territories. The French government expected that Upper Volta's abolition would facilitate the delivery of Mossi laborers throughout the AOF territory. Houphouët-Boigny, a deputy member of the French National Assembly, elected from the Côte d'Ivoire constituency (an overseas territory or colony), and future minister of the French government and then President of Côte d'Ivoire, supported the reestablishment of Upper Volta. As is frequently mentioned in archival documents, the French government paid close attention to Houphouët-Boigny's reaction to this issue.[22]

This was an influential factor in the reestablishment of Upper Volta. Houphouët-Boigny also anticipated that it would be challenging to win as much support for his election from the Voltaic people as from the Ivoirians if former Upper Volta regions remained within the Côte d'Ivoire colony. Moro Naba repeated and escalated his demand for the reestablishment of Upper Volta and also called on the non-Mossi chiefs of Ouahigouya (the colony of French Sudan)[23] and Fada N'Gourma (the colony of Niger) to work together for

---

the colonies to the Director-General of political, administrative, and social affairs of the AOF], June 21, 1946. CNA-BF.

[21] Secret telegram from the AOF, "Action anglaise sur le Moro Naba" ["British action on the Moro Naba"], June 20, 1946. CAN-BF.

[22] Lettre confidential du Gouverneur général de l'AOF au Ministre de l'Outre-Mer [Confidential Letter from Governor-General of the AOF to Minister of Oversea Territory (Colony)], July 1946. CNA-BF.

[23] Rapport confidentiel du Commandant de cercle de Ouahigouya p.i. au Gouverneur du Soudan Français [Confidential report from the Commandant of the Circle of Ouahigouya p.i. to the Governor of French Sudan], July 21, 1946. Archives national du Sénégal [National Archives of Senegal] (ANS).

the reestablishment of the Upper Volta colony[24] to escape dependence on the Côte d'Ivoire colony. Moro Naba needed the reestablishment of Upper Volta to send a deputy from the colony to Paris to champion Upper Volta's interests.[25]

A report on Upper Volta's reestablishment mentioned that reason for its abolition in 1932 was to provide a labor force to the Côte d'Ivoire and Niger colonies. It also mentioned the political reason for the reestablishment in 1947 that Ivoirian politicians, especially Houphouët-Boigny, preferred the separation of Upper Volta from the Côte d'Ivoire colony because of Houphouët-Boigny's election to the French National Assembly. Therefore, Upper Volta's reestablishment would not affect plantation owners (including himself) insofar as the labor force from Upper Volta was assured. This report was particularly concerned about the Fada cercle in Upper Volta, as the Fada region would be isolated in the reestablished Upper Volta colony after its return from the Niger colony.[26]

4.4. Border Disputes between Upper Volta (Burkina Faso) and Mali

4.4.1. Historical Overview of Border Disputes

Although Upper Volta (Burkina Faso since 1984) and Mali held countless meetings and dialogues aimed at resolving border disputes after their independence, the two countries fought two wars, as stated, in 1974 and 1985. The border and territorial disputes between the neighboring countries worsened and became increasingly complicated through the arbitral abolition (1932–1947) and the reestablishment of the Upper Volta colony by the French government.[27]

Consequently, Upper Volta and Mali had different ideas about the location of the sovereign border between the two countries. Through the bitter experiences of the two wars, Upper Volta (Burkina Faso) and Mali sued each other in the ICJ for violating the border. Border disputes damaged diplomatic relations and brought severe problems over economic activities for both landlocked

---

[24] Lettre du Moro-Naba, Empereur des Mossi à M. G. Bidault, Président du Conseil [Letter from Moro-Naba, Emperor of the Mossi to Mr. G. Bidault, President of the Council], September 4, 1946. ANS.

[25] Note sur la reconstitution éventuelle de la colonie de la Haute Volta, Direction Générale des affaires politiques, administratives, et sociales de l'AOF [Note on the reestablishment of the Colony of the Upper Volta, Direction-General of Political, Administrative, and Social Affairs of the AOF], January 30, 1947. CNA-BF.

[26] *Ibid.*

[27] Loi Nº 47-1707 du 4 septembre 1947, tendant rétablissement du territoire de la Haute Volta [Law No. 47-1707 of September 4, 1947, tending to reestablish the territory of Upper Volta]. CNA-BF.

countries. During the ICJ's judicial process, each country tried to verify the details of the border dispute to identify a solution.

> The two states have a common frontier of 1,380 kilometres according to Burkina Faso and 1,297 kilometres according to Mali, of which almost 900 kilometres according to Burkina Faso and almost 1,022 kilometres according to Mali have been successfully delimited by agreement between the Parties. The disputed area is defined by the Special Agreement as "a band of territory extending from the sector Koro (Mali) Djibo (Upper Volta) up to and including the region of the Béli". The Béli is the largest of the temporary watercourses in the region. It originates in the eastern slopes of the Hombori mountains and flows to the south-east before joining the Niger river outside the disputed area. (ICJ 1986d, 12)

According to the above-quoted ICJ report, the two countries were in agreement about roughly 70% of the border's delimitations. The border areas between the two countries were broadly located in pastoral areas with a Sahelian climate. In general, nomadic people would move and frequently cross the border to seek water and grass for their livestock. Water has been a truly precious natural resource in such a drought-prone region. The severe natural conditions complicated border negotiations owing to the issue of nomadic people's water management and their affiliation to either government.

The most contentious border region was located in the northeastern region of Upper Volta, which had been ruled under the French Sudan colony during the abolition period (1932–47).[28] People moved into the new colony unit, settled their villages, and developed their agro-pastoral activities in the former border area between French colonies. The abolition of Upper Volta made the border dispute between the two countries significantly more complicated after their independence.[29]

---

[28] The ICJ reported, "*Order No. 2728 AP* issued on *27 November 1935* by the Governor-General *ad interim* of French West Africa for the delimitation of the *cercles* of Bafoulabé, Bamako and Mopti (French Sudan). The last-named *cercle* bordered on the *cercle* of Ouahigouya, which was then a part of French Sudan and which reverted to Upper Volta as from 1947…. The text describes the eastern boundary of the Sudanese *cercle* of Mopti as being "a line running markedly north-east, leaving to the *cercle* of Mopti the villages of Yoro, Dioulouna, Oukoulou, Agoulourou, Koubo…" (ICJ 1986c, 10).

[29] The ICJ reported, "In its Memorial, Burkina Faso divided the disputed frontier into two sectors: the western part, described as the sector of the 'four villages', and the eastern sector, extending from the point with the co-ordinates 1°24'15" W and 14°43'45" N as far as the heights of N'Gouma. In its submissions however, throughout the proceedings, it divided the line it proposed into two sectors in relation to a different point (geographical

Therefore, the border question was complicatedly intertwined with questions of affiliations of villages, populations, and economic activities in the borderland.

Upper Volta was reconstituted in 1947 by the law 47-1707 of 4 September 1947, which rescinded outright the decree of 5 September 1932 that had abolished the colony of Upper Volta, and stated that the boundaries of "the re-established territory of Upper Volta" were to be "those of the former colony of Upper Volta on 5 September 1932". It was this reconstituted Upper Volta which subsequently obtained independence on 5 August 1960, and took the name of Burkina Faso in 1984. (ICJ 1986d, 19)

Although the law related to the reestablishment of the Upper Volta colony (1947) stipulated that the borders before the abolition in 1932 be readopted, the vague management of the territories and borders during the 15-year abolition period and the 13-year period from Upper Volta's reestablishment to its independence made issues more complicated between the two independent countries.[30] During the abolition period, borders and border-related issues

---

co-ordinates 0°40'47" W and 15°00'03" N); the Chamber will consider later what significance is to be attached to this point. For Mali, the disputed region can also be divided into two sectors: one extending from the village of Yoro to the pool of Kétiouaire, for which, according to Mali, a fairly precise delimitation exists, and the other from the pool of Kétiouaire to the heights of N'Gouma and the Kabia ford. In its Counter-Memorial, Burkina Faso preferred to adopt a division of the frontier into three sectors: the first from Dionouga to the point with the co-ordinates 1°24'15" W and 14°43'45" N (the region of the four villages), the second from the former point to mount Tabakarach (the Soum region), and the third from mount Tabakarach to the tripoint" (ICJ 1986d, 38).

[30] The ICJ reported, "To the south (from point Y to point Z), what in 1935 was the boundary between French Sudan and Niger was transformed in 1947, owing to the reincorporation of the *canton* of Aribinda and the Niger *cercle* of Dori into the restored colony of Upper Volta, into a mere administrative boundary within that colony between two *cantons* of the *cercle* of Dori. To the west, between point Y and point W, what had been in 1935 merely an administrative boundary between two Sudanese *cercles* (Mopti – including Bandiagara – and Ouahigouya) became once more the frontier between French Sudan and Upper Volta." (ICJ 1986d, 44) "In chronological order, the next regulative text that has to be mentioned is the decree of 5 September 1932, one of whose effects was the outright abrogation of the decree of 1 March 1919 which had created the colony of Upper Volta, and hence the abolition of that colony. The new decree, which came into force on 1 January 1933, also provided as follows: 'Art.2 – The *cercles* of Fada and Dori (except the *canton* of Aribinda) are annexed to the colony of Niger. The *cercle* of Ouahigouya, the *canton* of Aribinda within the *cercle* of Dori and that part of the *cercle* of Dedougou located on the left bank of the Black Volta are annexed to the colony of French Sudan...' By an Order of the Governor-General of French West Africa dated 17 November 1932, *the territories* of the colony of Upper Volta which had been annexed to French Sudan by the above-mentioned decree were reorganized as follows: '1. The *cercle* of Ouahigouya, at

among colonial administrative units became issues between the French Sudan and Niger colonies.[31]

A map is an essential material for border negotiations.[32] One factor that complicated the border negotiations between the two countries was the existence of maps made during the colonial time that showed borders demarcated differently, especially between Upper Volta and neighboring colonies ruled under the AOF. After Upper Volta and Mali gained independence, they claimed different maps for a basic understanding of the border.

---

present forming part of Upper Volta, and the *canton* of Aribinda, detached from the *cercle* of Dori, are to form a single unit under the name of the *cercle* of Ouahigouya, with its chief town at Ouahigouya...' This Order also came into force on 1 January 1933. It was in this administrative setting that an exchange of letters took place between the Governor-General of French West Africa and the Lieutenant-Governors of Niger and French Sudan, and this correspondence is relied upon by Burkina Faso" (ICJ 1986d, 42).

[31] The ICJ reported, "*Order dated 31 August 1927*, issued by the Governor-General *ad interim* of French West Africa, relating to the boundaries of the colonies of Niger and Upper Volta; this order was amended by an *erratum dated 5 October 1927.*... They disagree, however, regarding its validity; Mali claims that the Order and the erratum are invalidated by a factual error relating to the location of the heights of N'Gouma, so that Burkina Faso may not properly rely upon them" (ICJ 1986c, 10).

[32] The ICJ reported, "Two of the maps produced appear to be of special significance. These are the 1: 500,000 scale map of the colonies of French West Africa, 1925 edition, known as the Blondel la Rougery map, and the 1: 200,000 scale map of West Africa, issued by the French *Institut géographique national* (IGN) and originally published between 1958 and 1960" (ICJ 1986c, 9). "The Parties have devoted much attention to these, and Burkina Faso has referred expressly to them in its submissions. These are the 1: 500,000 scale map of the colonies of French West Africa, 1925 edition, compiled by the Geographical Service of French West Africa at Dakar and printed in Paris by Blondel la Rougery (reconnaissance map; compilation of the Hombori D 30 and Ansongo D 31 sheets); and 1: 200,000 scale map of West Africa, issued by the French Institut géographique national, which was originally published between 1958 and 1960 (Ansongo, In Tillit, Dori, Tera and Djibo sheets)" (ICJ 1986d, 34). "On 5 October 1927 an erratum to that Order was adopted, which replaced the above-quoted text with the following text: 'The boundaries of the colonies of Niger and Upper Volta are determined as follows: "A line starting at the heights of N'Gouma, passing through the Kabia ford (astronomic point), mount Arounskoye, mount Balébanguia to the west of the ruins of the village of Tokebangou, mount Doumafende and the astronomic marker of Tong-Tong; this line then heads south-east..."' There also exists a 1: 1,000,000 map, already mentioned, entitled 'French West Africa: New frontier of Upper Volta and Niger (according to the erratum of 5 October 1927 to the Order dated 31 August 1927)'. Mali has laid this map before the Chamber, but observes that it contains no information as to what official body compiled it or which administrative authority approved the line shown on it." (ICJ 1986d, 39).

4.4.2. Two Wars and Resolution between Burkina Faso (Upper Volta) and Mali

Although Burkina Faso (Upper Volta) and Mali went to war in 1974 and 1985, the two countries did attempt to resolve their border disputes through negotiations. Both wars were caused by border and territorial disputes concerning the northeastern regions of Upper Volta (southeastern regions of Mali). As soon as the two countries achieved independence, border negotiations repeatedly took place.[33]

Almost all African countries have experienced border disputes and concerns more or less with neighboring countries. Therefore, the OAU agreed with respect (no border modification attempt) to the borders inherited from the colonial administration in 1964 to avoid conflict and territorial adventures among the emerging African countries.

The essential natural border markings seasonally disappeared when the pools dried up during the drought season.[34] Both countries frequently highlighted the "pool of Soum" (*mare de Soum*).[35]

---

[33] The ICJ reported, "Thus, as early as 29 November 1961, they gave institutional shape to the regular meetings already held during the colonial period between the heads of the frontier districts, by establishing a 'mixed commission composed of the *chefs de circonscription*'. Subsequently, on 25 February 1964, they instituted a 'joint commission' comprising for each State a government delegate, a geographer, a topographer and the *commandants* of the frontier *cercles*, its task being to make proposals by 15 June 1964 'for the delimitation of the frontier on the basis of the preparatory work of the *chefs de circonscription*'. This commission was replaced by a 'standing joint commission' created on 8 May 1968, which comprised the Ministers of the Interior together with representatives of various ministries of both countries" (ICJ 1986d, 21).

[34] Rapport confidential, du commandant de cercle de Deuentza au Gouverneur de la région de Mopti [Confidential report, from the Deuentza circle commander to the Governor of the Mopti region], October 6, 1970. CNA-BF.

[35] The ICJ reported, "However that may be, it is obvious that the pool of Soum, situated some 24 kilometres to the east of the pool of Toussougou, requires particular examination. However, it is clear from the file that this pool, which was mentioned for the first time under this name in 1939, was thought to lie close to the meeting-point, not of the three *cercles* mentioned above of Mopti, Gourma-Rharous and Dori, but of the *cercles* of Mopti, Ouahigouya and Dori. A communication addressed by the *commandant de cercle* of Dori to the Governor of Niger on 18 December 1939 mentioned 'the pool of Sum' as being 'situated on the boundary of the *subdivision* of Douentza (*cercle* of Mopti) and of the *cercle* of Ouahigouya, to which it belongs'. On 7 July 1943, the *cercle* administrator of Dori asked the *commandant de cercle* of Mopti for information concerning the position of the pool of 'Souhoum' and 'the position in relation to the latter, or in relation to the village of Kouna, of the meeting point between the *cercles* of

According to a report on rural water resources dated 7 January 1957,
produced by Burkina Faso, the pool of Soum belongs to the category of
"major temporary pools which dry out in the dry season" and on 31
December of the same year, the report of a tour of inspection mentions
a "large pool of Soum which dries up... in March". The report notes that
"in view of the size of their herds, the Soum herdsmen are requesting the
construction of two field wells", and this work was recommended as a
"measure of the highest priority", on the ground that "Soum is the best
stockbreeding centre in the Djibo *subdivision* of the *cercle* of Ouahigouya,
in Upper Volta..." (ICJ 1986d, 81)

Thus, Upper Volta and Mali recognized different disputed border areas
(villages), which further complicated their negotiations and led to the first war
in 1974.[36]

The former President of Upper Volta, General Lamizana, noted this war
against Mali in his memoir. Lamizana was President of Upper Volta from 1966
to 1980. He noted that his country and Mali were exposed to this serious border
dispute only one year after their independence. The joint border meeting was
conducted in 1961. However, just after this meeting, Malian troops invaded the
territory of Upper Volta. Voltaic people were shot-killed by Malian border
officers in 1962 during their return from a village (Kouna-Habe) located on the
Malian side (Lamizana 1999, 299–301).

Mopti, Ouahigouya and Dori'" (ICJ 1986d, 77). "The Chamber must therefore observe
that if the pool of Kébanaire or that of Kétiouaire had, between 1935 and 1939, acquired
the new name of 'pool of Soum', it is likely that some reference to this would have
appeared in an administrative document, especially in view of the fact that the pool of
Kétiouaire, at least, was a sufficiently well known topographic feature in 1935 to be used
in defining the end-point of a *cercle* boundary" (ICJ 1986d, 79).

[36] The ICJ reported, "Following an armed conflict between the two countries which broke
out on 14 December 1974, appeals were made for conciliation, notably by the head of
State of Somalia, then President of the Organization of African Unity, and by the President
of Senegal. On 26 December 1974, the Presidents of Upper Volta, Mali, and Togo met at
Lomé and decided to set up a Mediation Commission composed of Togo, Niger, Guinea
and Senegal" (ICJ 1986d, 21).

Mali's drastic monetary policy change complicated the border issue. Mali left the CFA franc[37] system by establishing the Mali franc in 1962.[38] This affected the lives of borderland residents on both sides. At the border negotiation meeting in 1964, land possession, water use, and consecutive murders in the borderland regions became serious issues. The border disputes between the two countries were acknowledged as a serious concern by the OAU (Lamizana 1999, 301–03).

According to former President Lamizana, the regime turnover of Mali worsened the border dispute. In 1968, the first Malian President Keita was ousted by a coup d'état launched by General Traoré. After Traoré ascended to power by force, Mali became more aggressive in claiming its territory and relocated Malian people into the disputed border regions (Lamizana 1999, 303–04).

Meetings for resolving the border dispute were held in September 1974 and were broken off between the two countries. According to the former President of Upper Volta, in November 1974, Malian military officers violated Upper Volta's territory. The war started after an unsuccessful meeting between heads of state (December 14, 1974). Malian troops invaded Upper Volta's territory, reaching 15 km inside the border. The military battle ended only two days after the initial firing, resulting in a few deaths, with the acceptance of mediation from other leaders of West African countries, such as Togolese President Eyadéma (Lamizana 1999, 304–16).

Then, the two countries went to war again at the end of 1985 in a more severe battle than that in 1974. This second war was called "the Christmas War." This time, the military battle continued for five days and involved the mobilization of more massive weapons, which resulted in many casualties.[39]

A Burkinabe government report outlined the 1985 battle between Burkina Faso and Mali as follows.[40]

---

[37] CFA (Communauté financière africaine/African Financial Community) was established in 1945 as the common colonial currency in the French colonies. The exchange rate between the CFA and the French franc (later the Euro) was fixed at 50:1 (100:1 since 1994). Since its establishment, the French Ministry of Finance has indirectly continued influencing the decision-making regarding the CFA franc management.

[38] Mali returned to the CFA franc system in 1984.

[39] Government of Burkina Faso. (n.d.), *Litige frontalier Mali–Burkina Faso, Affrontement de noël 1985 une guerre absurd [Mali–Burkina Faso border dispute, Christmas confrontation in 1985, an absurd war]*

[40] *Litige frontalier Mali–Burkina Faso, Affrontement de noël 1985 une guerre absurd* [Mali–Burkina Faso border dispute, Christmas confrontation 1985 an absurd war], n.d. CNA-BF.

September 1983:	Both countries filed border complaints to the ICJ (The Hague)
September 1984:	Recommendation of compromise by the ICJ
November 24, 1985:	Military tension caused by kidnapping of Burkinabe resident by Malian troops in Soum
December 14:	Mali suspended diplomatic relations with Burkina Faso, accusing Burkinabe troops of occupying four Malian villages.
December 17:	Anti-Burkina Faso campaign in Mali
December 20:	Mediation of neighboring countries with President Sankara
December 24:	Message from Secretary-General of United Nations Firing by Burkinabe troops in Malian territories
December 25:	Firing by Malian troops
December 26:	Bombing of Sikasso by Burkinabe Mig
December 27:	France did not intervene in this war Malian troops attacked Sourou dam and Bobo-Dioulasso
December 29:	Fight in Kololo
December 30:	Signature for a ceasefire
January 10, 1986:	The ICJ required the withdrawal of troops within 20 days

However, the second war did not merely seem to be due to a border dispute but also due to more political and diplomatic reasons. The new military-revolutionary regime established in Burkina Faso in 1983, led by Captain Sankara, strongly displayed its revolutionary character. As Sankara was nicknamed "Africa's Che (Guevara)," he was very eager to export Burkina Faso's revolution to other African countries, especially neighboring countries. Seemingly, Sankara supported the opposition forces in Mali. Malian President Traoré was uncomfortable with Sankara's interventions. This political motive encouraged the Malian side's military attack (Jeune Afrique 2015c). Malian troops not only attacked the border region but went deeper inside Burkinabe territories with their (Soviet-made) Mig fighter jets.

According to a Malian government report of October 1985, these disputed areas—four villages called Diounouga, Oukoulourou, Agalourou, and Koubo—belonged to Mali (République du Mali 1985).[41] Burkina Faso highlighted the ambiguous border zone between Burkina Faso and Mali at independence in 1960. Some people were living on both sides of the border. Mali appealed for

---

[41] République du Mali. (1985). *Memoire: Affaire du differend frontalier Burkina Faso/Mali* (Vol. 2), 271–81.

recognition of the colonial border that had been modified in 1935 during Upper Volta's abolition.

> Among other measures, the Chamber is asking the Governments of Burkina Faso and Mali to withdraw their armed forces to such positions, or behind such lines as may, within twenty days of the delivery of the Order, be determined by agreement between the two Governments, ... (ICJ 1986b, 1)

Around ten days after the ceasefire, the ICJ called both countries to withdraw their troops to enable them to start the ICJ's charge to resolve the border dispute.[42]

The crucial question was which map made during the colonial era under the French authority the ICJ would use to make a ruling on the border dispute between the two countries.[43]

> A map, untitled and undated (according to Mali, it dates from 1900–1902 or 1909–1910), representing the Gourma and bearing the reference 12 D/6, and a sketch-map annexed to a 1923 census of villages belonging to the *canton* of Mondoro, on which Dioulouna is given, but not the other villages mentioned in Order 2728 AP. These other villages, in view of their position on the maps mentioned below, apparently should not appear on the aforementioned maps and sketch-maps since they lay

---

[42] The ICJ reported, "On Thursday 9 January 1986, at 10 a.m., a public sitting is to be held at the Peace Palace, The Hague, for the purpose of hearing representatives of Burkina Faso and Mali. The Governments of those countries are parties to the *Frontier Dispute* case which at their request was referred to a Chamber of the Court by a Special Agreement jointly filed on 14 October 1983" (ICJ 1986a, 1).

[43] The ICJ reported, "— A map of central Niger on the scale 1 : 1,000,000, compiled by Lieutenant Desplagnes in 1905, on which each of the five villages referred to in the Order is shown: Yoro, Dioulouna (spelt 'Dioukouna'), Oukoulou, Agoulourou, and Koubo. — A map of west Africa on the scale 1 : 2,000,000, sheet No.2: Timbuktu, published by the Geographical Service for the colonies in 1922, which shows Yoro, Dioukouna, Oukoulou (spelt 'Okolou') and Koubo, but not Agoulourou. However, a later edition of this map (1932) mentions only Yoro and Koubo. — The map of the colonies of French West Africa on the scale 1 : 500,000 (the Blondel la Rougery map of 1925) which shows Yoro, Oukoulou, Agoulourou and Koubo, but not Dioulouna. — The *Atlas des cercles de l'Afrique occidentale française* fascicle IV, map No.59, *cercle* of Ouahigouya (Geographical Service of French West Africa, 1926), which also shows Yoro, Oukoulou, Agoulourou and Koubo, but not Dioulouna. — A sketch-map of French Africa on the scale 1 : 1,000,000 (sheet ND-30, Ouagadougou) compiled in 1926, which shows Yoro, Oukoulou and Koubo, but not Dioulouna or Agoulourou" (ICJ 1986d, 55).

outside the *administrative* region covered by the maps and the sketch.
(ICJ 1986d, 55)

Burkina Faso requested the Chamber of the ICJ to acknowledge their border
according to the 1:200,000 scale map (1960 edition) of the French National
Geographic Institute (*Institut géographique national*) depicting that the villages of
Dioulouna, Oukoulou, Agoulourou, and Koubo had been located in Burkinabe
territory (ICJ 1986d, 10–11).

However, Mali made the following different claims.

The Government of the Republic of Mali submits as follows:
To state that the frontier line between the Republic of Mali and Burkina
Faso in the disputed area runs through the following points:
—   Lofou,
—   the mosque-shaped enclosure situated 2 kilometres to the north of
       Diguel,
—   a point situated 3 kilometres to the south of Kounia,
—   the Selba baobab,
—   the Tondigaria,
—   Fourfaré Tiaiga,
—   Fourfaré Wandé,
—   Gariol,
—   Gountouré Kiri,
—   a point to the east of the pool of Kétiouaire, having the following
       geographical co-ordinates, longitude o° 44'47" W, latitude 14°
       56'52" N
—   the pool of Raf Naman (ICJ 1986d, 11)

The ICJ concluded and offered its intermediary proposition after 11 months
of judicial charge. Ultimately, the ICJ proposed that both countries accept
sharing the pool, delimiting a border on the pool, and dividing it into two parts
on an equal surface.

In order to achieve an equitable solution along these lines, on the basis
of the applicable law, the Chamber finds that account must be taken, in
particular, of the circumstances in which the *commandants* of two
adjacent *cercles*, one in Mali and the other in Upper Volta, recognized in
a 1965 agreement, not endorsed by the competent authorities, that the
pool should be shared. It concludes that the pool of Soum must be
divided in two in an equitable manner. The line should, therefore, cross
the pool in such a way as to divide its maximum area during the rainy
season equally between the two States.(ICJ 1986c, 14)

4.5. Conclusion

This chapter revisited the history surrounding the border issue and disputes between Burkina Faso (Upper Volta) and Mali (French Sudan) as a symbolic case of Africa's border issues and disputes by referring to colonial archival documents. Almost all African countries have suffered from border-originated problems and concerns since their independence. Consequently, border issues have continued to politically and economically threaten the security of African countries.

In the twenty-first century, border issues remain a contentious matter in every African country. Therefore, understanding such issues is crucial for understanding the challenges facing Africa's domestic politics and international relations. Thus, this chapter was intended to revisit and examine the origin of a border dispute on the African continent.

Border management has become more of a focal issue for economic integration at the continental level since the African Continental Free Trade Area (AfCFTA) agreement was concluded among African countries in 2019. As the AU recognizes borders as bridges (no longer barriers; AUBP 2013) among African states, borders and borderland regions are attracting more attention from policymakers and international organizations. Consequently, cross-border engagement and cooperation hold greater promise for each African country.

This chapter examined the border history between Burkina Faso (Upper Volta) and Mali (French Sudan) as a case study. Both neighboring countries are landlocked. Therefore, the border dispute affects their economic and political security more severely than other African countries possessing their own coastal lines and ports. In recent years, both countries' borders have attracted more attention from the international community owing to regional security concerns. This region has become more destabilized, particularly since Mali's coup d'état occurred in 2012. Due to the power vacuum caused by the coup, jihadist groups could expand their activities from the northern regions of Mali to more southern regions, including neighboring countries, such as Burkina Faso and Côte d'Ivoire, although United Nations peacekeeping operations have been conducted over the years.

The insurrection of 2014 and (failed) coup attempt of 2015 in Burkina Faso encouraged jihadist groups' activities. The insecurity of both countries' borderlands has already become a grave regional security concern for West Africa and the international community. Therefore, Africa's borders are becoming more significant for understanding current and future security, trade, and people's lives. However, the context of African border issues is not unique, despite common experiences such as Burkina Faso's case. Therefore, we must understand the historical origin of the current African borders.

This chapter reflected on the origin of contemporary Africa's border issues by revisiting border disputes between Burkina Faso and Mali. In resolving their border disputes, the two countries have progressed in their cross-border cooperation in the borderlands (Chapter 5). Cross-border cooperation is required to strengthen peace and security cooperation for both countries. Severe political instabilities in both countries will inevitably undermine the achievements of their cross-border cooperation and borderland security. The political disaster that occurred in both countries is regrettable. Even six decades after the Year of Africa (1960), border issues are still significant concerns for African states. However, the African borders also provide potential opportunities to encourage free trade on the African continent (including island nations). The African borders continue to be focal points for development, nation-building, security, and trade in Africa's future.

Chapter 5

Borders and Regional Security in Local Governments' Cooperation in West Africa: Boundaries and Bridges[1]

Like in Europe, peripheral-border regions are usually neglected and border populations' potential is not capitalized on, neither in socio-cultural nor economic terms. Cross-border cooperation aims at solving those problems of border populations including those of minorities. (WABI 2007a, 30)

5.1 Introduction

This chapter aims to reflect on the border (political and geographical boundary) issues in Africa by examining international cooperation among local governments and issues relating to regional security in West African countries, principally focusing on Burkina Faso. According to recent political history in West African countries, a domestic political dispute or conflict is likely to become a regionalized concern across national borders.

West Africa is known as the region where people have collectively moved and exchanged through long-distance trade and the immigration of peoples, such as Mandingo and Hausa merchants, Fulani people, and military troops, who have long enjoyed water transportation via the Niger River, dating back to the time of the great ancient empires.

Conflicts in Côte d'Ivoire and Mali in the twenty-first century have severely affected neighboring countries in terms of the economy, politics, and security. In Burkina Faso, President Compaoré was forced to step down unexpectedly in 2014, after 27 years of authoritarian rule, because of the huge popular insurgency against his trial of constitutional change for his third presidential

---

[1] This chapter was originally published in the journal of the International Studies Association of Ritsumeikan University (Kyoto, Japan): Iwata, T. (2016a). Borders and Regional Security in Local Governments' Cooperation in West Africa: Case Studies in Burkina Faso. *Ritsumeikan Annual Review of International Studies, 15*, 1–25.

term.[2] This incident created a serious political vacuum in terms of regional security in West Africa. This unforeseen political turnover of Burkina Faso was a cause of great concern for the French and US governments regarding regional security in West Africa, especially considering the volatile situation in northern Mali.

Unfortunately, this concern materialized in attacks on hotels and cafés by an armed group in Ouagadougou, Burkina Faso's capital city, in January 2016. This terror attack was orchestrated by a group affiliated with Al Qaeda, Al Qaeda, in the Islamic Maghreb (AQIM) (BBC 2016; Jeune Afrique 2016a, 2016b; Kindo 2016; RFI 2016).[3] The group is similar to other armed jihadist groups, which are generally based in northern Mali and easily cross the borders of the Sahelian countries. This group crossed the border from Mali to Burkina Faso to carry out this terror attack. In addition, Boko Haram has not only attacked cities and abducted people in northern Nigeria but also crossed national borders to expand its aggression into Cameroon, Chad, and Niger. Thus, Boko Haram is

---

[2] Compaoré changed the Constitution for the first time in 1997 to remove the limitation on the presidential term. However, this constitutional modification was met with huge protests and the assassination of Norbert Zongo. Zongo was a widely famous journalist who had investigated an arbitrary murder caused by François Compaoré, the president's younger brother. Compaoré had to accept the reinsertion of the presidential term limitation into the constitution (Article 37) in 2004. Article 37 limits the president to two terms (five years in each term), for a total of ten years. After this constitutional change, the presidential election was held under the new Constitution in 2005. Compaoré was re-elected. Compaoré tried again to remove Article 37 to eternalize his power before the end of his second term in 2015. Under such tense situations, in October 2014, National Assembly members tried to force the adoption of a proposition to organize a constitutional change. The seats in the National Assembly were massively dominated by the members of Compaoré's party (*Congrès pour la démocratie et le progress*, CDP). On October 30, 2014, the day of the National Assembly vote, a massive protest took place against the constitutional violation. Hundreds of thousands of demonstrators joined in the protests in Ouagadougou and other big cities. Demonstrators started attacking and setting fire to state institutions, such as the National TV broadcaster's office and houses of members of parliament and dignitaries of the Compaoré regime, including the National Assembly building itself. Despite interventions from security forces, these demonstrations could not be stopped. President Compaoré announced that he was abandoning the constitutional modification and announced his retirement at the end of his final term at the end of 2015. His speech was broadcast from a private TV station because the national TV station had been occupied by demonstrators. However, this speech failed to appease the demonstrators; instead, it made them accelerate their actions. Demonstrators began demanding President Compaoré's immediate resignation (Iwata 2016b, 147–48).

[3] After Mali (November 2015) and Burkina Faso, Grand-Bassam, a touristic town located 40 km from Abidjan, was attacked by the AQIM in March 2016.

no longer a domestic security problem for Nigeria; it has become a regional and continental concern.

Robert Kaplan (2012, 352–53) mentions the following:

> Whereas *borders* indicate passport controls and fixed divisions of sovereignty, *frontiers* indicate a pre-modern world of vaguer, more informal, overlapping divisions. The Great Middle East is moving away from a world of borders and toward one of frontiers... Again, this is increasingly a geographer's world, where state borders erode and vaguer frontiers become more relevant.

The border between sovereign states is not necessarily a barrier for extremist groups; rather, it is occasionally a convenient, permeable membrane behind which they can defend themselves. On the contrary, the border is impenetrable for African states' "national" armies without international coordination.

In addition to border and security issues, this chapter focuses on decentralization. Decentralization has been one of the most formidable challenges in terms of governance in African countries since the democratization process started in the 1990s. Therefore, there is a need to examine the international cooperation and politics of local governments in the borderlands since these states began tackling democratization in order to understand regional security and border issues. We cannot expect to find an efficient solution to problems and conflicts related to borders without considering the role of local actors inhabiting the borderlands, because the lives and interests of the local people are closely intertwined with questions regarding borders and security. However, the existing frameworks for border and security management might be insufficient for addressing this question. It is meaningful to focus on the local actors because the borders have changed in character and become vaguer in terms of their orientation.

Burkina Faso is located in the center of West Africa and has a border spanning 3,611 km that it shares with Benin (386 km of the border), Côte d'Ivoire (545 km), Ghana (602 km), Mali (1,325 km), Niger (622 km), and Togo (131 km). It has faced border disputes with these neighboring countries because of the ambiguous administrative borders drawn by the French colonial authority (examined in Chapter 4). Like other landlocked countries, Burkina Faso faces serious difficulties in terms of its economy and security.

However, the political leadership of Burkina Faso has not only suffered from border issues but also profited from them. During the Compaoré administration (1987–2014), he profited from the geographical location of Burkina Faso by intervening in other African countries because of the political instability of other West African countries (Journal du Jeudi 2010). For instance, the Compaoré Administration made profits from civil wars or conflicts in Sierra

Leone and Côte d'Ivoire while covertly supporting the illegal diamond and arms trades (African Arguments 2012; BBC 2000) while acting as the intermediary of peace talks in West Africa.

Figure 5.1. Borders of Burkina Faso

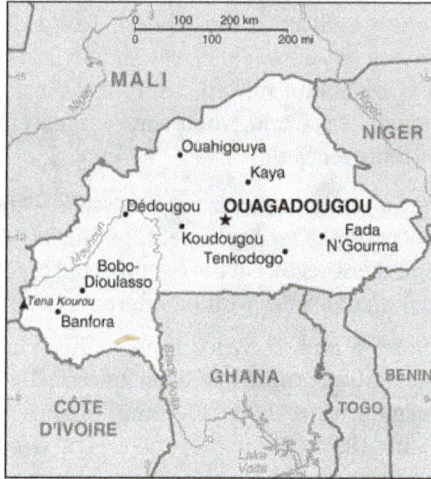

Source: Central Intelligence Agency (2016)

This chapter attempts to decode the security issues in West Africa by examining questions about borders and the cross-border cooperation of local governments through case studies in Burkina Faso and neighboring countries.

5.2. Rethinking Borders and Security in Africa

5.2.1. Contemporary History

Since independence, national borders have been a serious national security concern for African countries. These are colonial borders that the sovereign African states retained, and despite the claim that these borders were delimited or imposed by European colonizers, African countries have not been able to draw more authentic borders.

The Organisation of African Unity (OAU) stipulated the principle of respect for existing borders in 1964, and its charter advocates respect for the sovereignty and territory of African countries (Touval 1972, 42, 86). This principle of maintaining the status quo of national borders was succeeded by the African Union (AU), founded in 2002. Thus, African states have adopted this principle in attempting to deal with domestic and international disputes caused by border-related problems. Many African countries have suffered from conflicts with rebel groups fighting for separatist movements, such as Katanga

(DR Congo), Cabinda (Angola), and Casamance (Senegal), or reunification movements for divided compatriots, such as the Great Somali movement (spreading over Somalia, Djibouti, Ethiopia, and Kenya) and Ewe unification movement (Ghana and Togo). Eritrea (in 1993) and South Sudan (in 2011) achieved their independence after long and painful struggles. These two cases are the only cases of independence that separated existing African countries and created new borders.

African states have recognized that a modification of state borders might open Pandora's box and destabilize each African state (Touval 1972, 83). In the early 1960s, the issue of the independence of Eritrea from Ethiopia divided African countries into two blocs: the Casablanca group and the Monrovia group. The OAU called on the African countries to respect the given borders that the newly born African countries had inherited from the former European colonizers. After the results of the January 2011 referendum, South Sudan achieved independence in July 2011. The international community welcomed this newest case of independence.

In general, armed conflicts have begun inside an African country and then occasionally crossed borders into neighboring countries. Despite severe border disputes, there have been few cases of war breaking out between national armies because African armies have tended to intervene in internal affairs, rather than fight foreign armies. Therefore, the wars that took place between Burkina Faso (Upper Volta)[4] and Mali in 1974 and 1985 owing to border disputes do not necessarily evince the general character of armed conflicts in the history of postcolonial Africa.

Colonial borders were accepted as international and official borders among the African states upon independence. While the border issue might be "old," it has been repeatedly renewed for young African states. Borders have not only brought about territorial disputes but also political concern about struggles for survival during conflicts that have created massive numbers of refugees. Even in conflict-free (but not necessarily peaceful) times, the issues relating to borders are always very sensitive ones of anti-government rebel forces' activities, smuggling in the borderlands, and regional integration.

Borders certainly existed among African states in the pre-colonial era. Throughout Africa's long history, many kingdoms and chieftaincies were established and perished. However, the governing bodies at that time did not necessarily delimit strict geographical borders. Traditionally, the rule in peripheral regions was more geographically vague. Even during the colonial

---

[4] Upper Volta (Haute-Volta) changed its name to Burkina Faso in 1984 under the revolutionary regime led by Captain Sankara.

period, massive movements of people and ethnic groups crossed the colonial borders repeatedly to escape despotic rule (Herbst 2000, 88).

The delimitation of colonial borders can be divided into two categories. The first category comprises the borders that were demarcated by an agreement among European countries. These were the international borders between European colonies. The second category consists of the borders drawn inside the colonies (Touval 1972, 4)—that is, the domestic borders. The colonial borders have not only divided ethnic groups and living areas but have also created new identities and aroused new interests in African people (Nugent 2002, 273).

On the one hand, globalization is recognized as a basic feature in the contemporary world. People, capital, and information have been crossing national borders on a large scale and instantly. On the other hand, borders have not faded under globalization; they continue to exert a significant influence on people's lives, especially in borderlands. Borders continue to create outsiders beyond their limits, and not only in a geographical sense. The borders have influenced and edified the identities of communities and individuals and have constituted a base of political conflict. These aspects are displayed in the formation process of sovereign states. However, European countries drew artificial borders through few consultations with African authorities and African people.

5.2.2. Borders and Security in Burkina Faso and Neighboring Countries

The final border beacon (*la borne* in French) of delimitation between Burkina Faso (Upper Volta until 1984) and Mali was eventually established in 2010. The inauguration ceremony commemorating the peaceful resolution of the border dispute was attended by representatives of both countries. After long and painstaking negotiations between Burkina Faso and Mali, with the support of the OAU (transformed into the AU in 2002) and the Economic Community of West African States (ECOWAS) and accepting the judgment of the International Court of Justice (ICJ 1986), the two countries finally concluded their border agreement. Thus, the border dispute between Burkina Faso and Mali was finally resolved 50 years after their independence (ICJ 2013; Jan 2015; Jeune Afrique 2015a; Le monde 2015).[5]

---

[5] In 2015, Burkina Faso and Niger accepted the proposition of the ICJ to modify their shared border and consequently resolve a dispute over 18 villages.

Figure 5.2. Resolution of the border dispute between Burkina Faso and Mali

FRONTIERE BURKINA-MALI

Finies les barrières, place aux passerelles

La dernière borne de démarcation de la frontière Burkina–Mali a été posée le 29 janvier 2010 à Hèrémakono, village malien situé à 6 km de Kologo, 51 de Orodara et 126 de Bobo Dioulasso. La cérémonie, co-organisée par les deux pays, a permis aux ministres Clément Sawadogo de l'Administration territoriale et de la Décentralisation et son homologue malien, le général Kafougouna Koné, de procéder à l'acte historique qui marque la matérialisation totale de cette frontière commune longue de 1303 km.

Par Serge COULIBALY

Jeudi 29 janvier 2010. Jour de joie, de gloire mais aussi et surtout un jour mémorable pour le Burkina et le Mali. Les 1303 km de frontière qui séparent ces deux pays de l'Afrique de l'Ouest ne devraient plus connaître de litige. Le processus de délimitation de cette frontière commune enclenché en 1990 suite au verdict de la Cour internationale de justice le 22 décembre 1986, est arrivé à son terme le 29 janvier 2010 par la pose symbolique de la dernière borne. En

La pose symbolique de cette dernière borne marque la matérialisation totale de la frontière Burkina-Mali

Source: *Le Pays* (Burkina Faso, 2010)

During the first war between Burkina Faso and Mali in 1974, the name of a young soldier, future President Sankara, was diffused among the people of Upper Volta because he had bravely fought in Malian territory. This war brought Sankara much admiration from the Voltaic (Burkinabe) people. During this war, Sankara met his comrade Compaoré (President, 1987–2014). This war gave young officers an opportunity to join in a political game and finally establish the revolutionary regime (1983–87) in Burkina Faso through a military coup d'état led by Sankara and Compaoré. The meeting of young comrades continues to influence Burkinabe politics.

Although Upper Volta retained its colonial borders, like other African countries, its border-related situation was more complicated because it was established as a colonial administrative unit (*Circonscription administrative*) under *Afrique occidentale française* (AOF, French West Africa) in 1919, then abolished once in 1932, but finally re-established in 1947.[6] Upon re-establishing this colonial unit, some parts of the colonial administrative borders inside the AOF remained vague until independence. Upper Volta's border was buffeted by the shift of French colonial rule. This capricious re-establishment of the administrative unit in the French colony brought about more complicated and controversial border issues between Upper Volta (Burkina Faso) and neighboring countries after their independence.

---

[6] The colony of Upper Volta was divided into three parts and absorbed into the three French West African colonies of Côte d'Ivoire, French Soudan (currently Mali), and Niger from 1932 to 1947.

5.3. Local Government Cooperation in the Decentralization Process

5.3.1. Local Governance in the Era of Globalization

Decentralization began in the mid-1990s in African countries, and it is appropriate to reconsider this process, as it has exposed its malfunction over the last two decades. Decentralization is the process of financial, human, and technical devolution from the central government to local governments to empower the latter. Although numerous studies have been done on decentralization in Africa, they have principally focused on administrative reform while neglecting political dynamism. Decentralization is the process of redefining the roles and responsibilities of central and local governments. Therefore, decentralization is essentially political reform (Saito 2008, 284).

At the dawn of the decentralization process, Western donor countries expected that decentralization would lead to an improvement in local governance in African countries. However, the expectations for decentralization seemed to be inflated as a panacea-like reform without sufficient reflection on the historical, social, and political realities in each country. In addition, the international community in foreign aid naively expected that decentralization would promote democratization at the local level and spread to national politics. These discourses have been based more on ideological ideas than on real experiences on the ground.

Decentralization certainly increased resources and affected the power balance in local politics (Iwata 2011). A few researchers have focused on the impact of decentralization on elections in Africa. One reason for this is that few African countries have repeatedly held local elections since the decentralization reform was initiated. Due to the lack of financial, human, and technical resources in the central government of a developing country, the local governments may not have expected sufficient devolution of these resources. After local elections were held to complete the decentralization process, the newly elected representatives in the local governments faced demands for local development from the residents. Therefore, the local governments needed to establish direct and close relationships with foreign local governments in order to supplement the above-mentioned resources. Consequently, decentralization stimulated the international activities of local governments in Africa.

In addition, quite a few studies on decentralization in Africa have examined the security issue. The framework of the international cooperation of local governments, called *coopération décentralisée* (decentralized cooperation), between France and French-speaking African countries, has been thoroughly promoted by the French government working with French local governments and other European donor countries, such as Germany and Italy.[7] Decentralized cooperation is the cooperative framework of local governments with a foreign/domestic local partner to realize common interests (French Foreign Ministry 2007). Therefore, many local governments in Africa have concluded cooperation agreements with non-African local governments as well as those of neighboring African countries. As decentralization progressed, the cross-border local cooperation became more meaningful regarding regional security and the socioeconomic development of borderlands.

5.3.2. Burkina Faso and Neighboring Countries

Burkina Faso was a strategically important country for France to promote the local government cooperation policy in Africa as well as regional security. France has appreciated Burkina Faso as a model of decentralization[8] and inter-local government cooperation.[9] As the satirical neologism *"Françafrique"*[10] suggests, Africa has always been an indispensable resource for France to

---

[7] France is the aggressive promoter of local government cooperation (decentralized cooperation) in Africa (principally in francophone Africa). Local government cooperation is not only a cooperation tool but also a "value" for European countries that is based on their experience of reconciliation after World War II. Local government cooperation was launched between French and German local governments to establish a multilateral network of two nations for sustainable peace. Furthermore, local government cooperation was developed through the integration process of the European Union. Local government cooperation is literally the cooperation among local governments and is not limited to cultural exchange with the sister-city framework. Local government cooperation was stimulated and expanded through the decentralization process that enabled local governments to conduct more direct and international cooperation with foreign local governments in pursuit of fulfilling local interests.

[8] Since the decentralization process started in 1995, 359 local units (49 urban, 302 rural, 8 particular *arrondissements* in Ouagadougou and Bobo-Dioulasso), known as *communes*, and 13 regions were established in Burkina Faso. A *commune* is a basic unit of local administration equivalent to a city or town. The *arrondissement* is an administrative unit as the ward in the commune of special status and allowed similar status to a commune. Burkina Faso inherited the French system of local governance, like other French-speaking African countries. The law related to local government (Code general des collectivités territoriales, 2004) stipulated the devolution from central to local government. The first full-scale local elections in Burkina Faso took place in 2006.

[9] The history of local government cooperation in Burkina Faso started with the sister-city agreement between Ouagadougou and Loudun (France) in 1967. More than 120 agreements of local government cooperation were concluded between the French and Burkinabe local governments until 2007.

[10] *Françafrique* is a satirical neologism expressing complex feelings that are critical of the close and corrupt relationship between France and the former French colonies established through very personal connections among the leaders and elites. See Verschave (2000).

maintain its diplomatic status within the international community as a globally influential actor.

The Association of Municipalities of Burkina Faso (*Association des municipalités du Burkina Faso*, AMBF) was founded as the main body to promote local government cooperation activities in Burkina Faso. It has been principally supported by France and Canada (more specifically, the Government of Quebec). The leading French coordinator of the local government cooperation is *Cités unies France* (CUF). The Burkinabe government established the special institution, *Maison de coopération décentralisée* (MCD), in 2003, which would later be absorbed into the AMBF.

Figure 5.3. Session on local government triangular cooperation (The National Congress of Local Governments in Burkina Faso [*Journée de la commune burkinabé*] organized by AMBF)

Source: Author (December 2007, Ouagadougou, Burkina Faso)

The second international meeting of *Franco-Burkinabe coopération décentralisée* was held in Ouagadougou in December 2007 with 1,500 participants from Burkina Faso (including 359 mayors), France, Germany, Italy, Canada, Niger, Senegal, Mali, and Burundi. This event comprised two general meetings, three sections, and nine group discussions over the course of two days. The local government triangular cooperation among Burkinabe–French–German local governments[11] was proposed by the German government.

The border dispute between Burkina Faso and Mali drove them to fight (Chapter 4). Therefore, both countries recognized the importance of international and

---

[11] The trial of triangular cooperation was launched by Burkinabe, French, and German local governments. Burkina Faso is the pilot model country in terms of multilateral local partnerships in Africa. Subsequently, German, Italian, and Swiss local governments began working on a triangle cooperation.

local cooperation. The political instability in Mali after the coup d'état of 2012 certainly affected the political situation of Burkina Faso. The terrorist attack that occurred in January 2016 in Ouagadougou offers the most significant case of border security issues between the two countries because these armed forces entered Burkinabe territory via Mali, thereby crossing the border to carry out this attack. Political instability allows the expansion of the activities of such jihadist groups. Before this serious incident, Samoroguan, a town located in the western region of Burkina Faso and 30 km from the border with Mali, had been attacked by an armed group in October 2015 (Jeune Afrique 2015b). The Burkinabe government had to acknowledge the importance of border security in its relations with Mali to maintain its sovereignty and national security.

Similar to Burkina Faso, Mali is a landlocked country, surrounded by 7,243 km of land borders with seven neighboring countries. Due to the Ivorian crisis that occurred in the 2000s, Mali temporarily lost its free access to the port of Abidjan,[12] one of the most important ports in West Africa, where 70% of goods are transported from/to Mali.

Figure 5.4. SKBo area

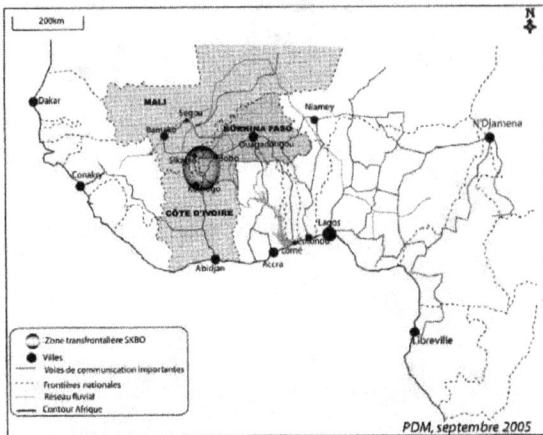

Source: Dahou et al. (2007, 16)

The northern territory had been practically the area outside the efficient control of the Malian central government even before the AQIM and other jihadist forces expanded their influence in the Sahel region. Therefore, Mali needs a good neighbor policy to handle this emergency situation. Mali has

---

[12] As the Ivorian crisis intensified, Mali had to seek an alternative supply route, which was longer and costlier, such as from/to Dakar, Conakry, even Lome, or Cotonou, passing Burkina Faso. During my fieldwork in Benin in 2006, I watched many Malian trucks and tank lorries travel. Mali had to pay additional costs for its economic activities.

stressed local government cooperation among the local governments of the borderland. The cooperation between Mopti (Mali)–Ouahigouya (Burkina) and Sikasso (Mali)–Korhogo (Côte d'Ivoire)–Bobo Dioulasso (Burkina), called SKBo, is a remarkable example of the cross-border local government cooperation for Mali.

Figure 5.5. International meeting for local government cooperation in Mali

Source: Author (December 2008, Bamako, Mali)

The Association of Municipalities of Mali (*Association des municipalités du Mali*, AMM) is the main organizer of local government cooperation. The author attended the meeting for local government cooperation held in Bamako in December 2008, organized by the AMM under the supervision of President Touré. Mali was the second largest base of local government cooperation for France after Burkina Faso.

5.3.3. Interests of France in Local Government Cooperation in Africa

France has been keen to sustain its influence on its former African colonies, covering a wide range of interests, including cultural, economic, educational, military, and political aspects. In addition, Burkina Faso is located at the center of French-speaking West Africa. When the terrorist attack occurred in Ouagadougou in January 2016, French troops were immediately dispatched to intervene against the armed group and to control the situation in cooperation with Burkinabe and US troops (Jeune Afrique 2016c). France's stake in the decentralization and local government cooperation in Africa is not only related to socioeconomic activities; it is also important for international strategy and security. The following is the French government's definition of decentralized cooperation (*Coopération décentralisée*). The National Committee of decentralized cooperation (*Comité nationale de la coopération décentralisée*, CNCD) was set up in the French foreign ministry (*Ministères des affaires étrangères et européennes*; L. 1112-6, Article 134, 1992):

> Decentralized cooperation is the ensemble of actions for international cooperation with an agreement in the objectives of common interest between French and foreign local governments. Decentralized cooperation takes place in diverse forms such as sister-city, development program, and technical exchanges. Decentralized cooperation is speculated in the largest framework of local government's foreign action by the circular of Prime Minister, announced on May 26, 1983.[13]

Decentralized cooperation is not only for the sake of local development but also a strategic tool for diversifying French diplomacy in Africa. The French government needs to involve more French citizens in development assistance in Africa and to increase the support for the French government's African policy. Decentralized cooperation is secondary diplomacy[14] for the French government to maintain its influence in Africa, which allows France to keep its status as an influential actor in the international community.

---

[13] French Ministry of the Interior & Ministry of Foreign Affaires. (2001). Circular of April 20, 2001, on decentralized cooperation of French local authorities and their groups with foreign local authorities and their groups (*Circulaire du 20 avril 2001 sur la coopération décentralisée des collectivités territoriales françaises et de leurs groupements avec des collectivités territoriales étrangères et leurs groupements*). https://www.senat.fr/ct/ct04-02/ct04-0228.html (accessed September 20, 2023).

[14] France and Germany initiated local government cooperation after the end of World War II to avoid another tragic war. Both countries were confident that local government cooperation would establish strong friendships between the two nations and ensure a diversified communication channel that would keep the peace. This local government cooperation has developed for Europe not only in terms of friendships but also in terms of achieving national and regional security goals.

Figure 5.6. Strategic framework for international cooperation in the French government

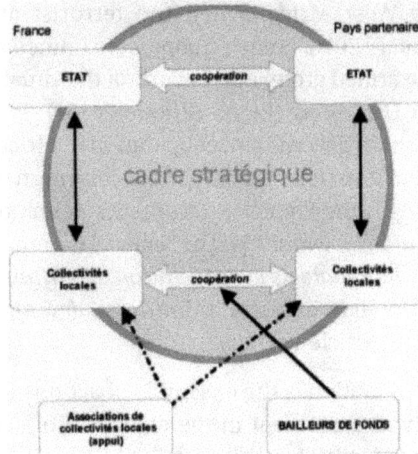

Source: Coopération décentralisée et développement urbain (2007, 56)

Figure 5.8. above depicts the scheme of decentralized cooperation. It is a mixed cooperation between states (*Etat*) and local governments (*Collectivités locales*). *Cités unies France* is the coordinator organization for the local government cooperation between the French and foreign local governments (Foreign Ministry of France 2012a).[15] The French Foreign Ministry provides financial support to the French local governments cooperating with the local governments in Africa. In total, the French Foreign Ministry funds 50% of the total amount for a project undertaken by a French local government (Foreign Ministry of France 2012b). This is called "co-finance" (*co-financement*).

5.4. Border Issues and Regional Security in Local Government Cooperation

5.4.1. Decentralization and Cross-Border Cooperation

This part focuses on local involvement in socioeconomic development and security issues in the borderlands.

> Country's sovereignty stops at the border. That means: sovereign rights of two States meet at the border, but no State has the sole power to act across this border. Therefore, cross-border structures are needed, ideally at the regional/local level acting as drivers of co-operation. (WABI 2007a, 31)

---

[15] In total, 3,800 French local governments have participated in the local government cooperation, representing 8,000 projects.

Border control and regional security can be carried out only through international and regional cooperation among neighboring states. There are residents living on both sides of the border, who frequently cross the border to undertake their daily activities. The cross-border cooperation is not only expected to establish and develop the socioeconomic relations in the neighboring communities but also to ensure national and regional security. After African countries began implementing the decentralization reform, the local governments were expected to play a key role in the economic development and improvement of the life of the local residents through the devolution process from the central government to the local governments (OECD–SWAC 2010, 27). Thus, the local governments eagerly sought foreign partners. Therefore, international cooperation between local governments was stimulated in the decentralization process. It has been indispensable for advancing international cooperation among local governments in the borderlands, especially with neighboring communities across their borders, in order to carry out economic development and strengthen the security of the borderlands.

People living in a borderland are linked socioeconomically and culturally (OECD–SWAC 2010, 8). The concept of a cross-border region was proposed by Malian President Konaré in 2002, and cross-border cooperation has expanded throughout West Africa. Consequently, local governments have concluded sister cities and other agreements.[16] Civil society associations encourage that local people resolve conflict through a mediation process. Some other functions of these agreements are that health centers coordinate the use of their resources, schools accept young students living on the other side of their border, livestock breeders employ transhumance corridors, and traders have established border markets (WABI 2005, 7).

At the workshop on border cooperation held in Ouagadougou in July 2003, WABI (West African Borders and Integration or *Frontières et intégration en Afrique de l'Ouest* in French) was established. WABI was supported by the National Division of Borders Mali (a state organization), ENDA–Diapol (an NGO), and OECD–SWAC (an international organization)[17] for funding (WABI 2005, 2).

---

[16] Organizations for local cooperation work together, such as the Mali Association of Municipalities (AMM), the Burkina Faso Association of Municipalities (AMBF), the Municipal Development Partnership (PDM), the International Association of Francophone Mayors (AIMF), *Cités unies France* (CUF), the Association of European Border Regions (AEBR), and the Cross-border Operational Mission (MOT) (OECD Sahel and West Africa Club 2010, 19).

[17] According to OECD–SWAC (2010), "The decentralisation process is an ongoing one which is subject to supervision on the part of support programmes with the backing of

5.4.2. Cross-Border Local Cooperation

The SKBo region is recognized as the most hopeful and attractive case of triangular cross-border cooperation in West Africa. Each country in this triad has peripheral areas (Dahou et al. 2007, 15), including the cities of Sikasso (Mali), Korhogo (Côte d'Ivoire), and Bobo Dioulasso (Burkina Faso). SKBo contains 3.5 million inhabitants and covers an area of 115,000 km². This cross-border area was built through the kingdoms (of Kong, Kénédougou, and Gwiriko) and the colonial period. The kingdom of Kénédougou had Sikasso as its capital and ruled most part of the SKBo region between the seventeenth and eighteenth centuries (Yatta 2011, 2).

The intertwining historical, geographical, and commercial aspects of this border region make it a dynamic area (Dahou et al. 2007, 16). The SKBo region has been a space of close political, economic, and religious ties, creating a hub of trade, information, and finance (Dahou et al. 2007, 40). This area is at the heart of the production of cotton, cereals, fruits, vegetables, and animal husbandry. The port of Abidjan in Côte d'Ivoire includes indispensable infrastructure for the economies of Burkina Faso and Mali because they are landlocked countries (PDM 2006, 8).

The crisis that occurred in Côte d'Ivoire at the beginning of the twenty-first century severely damaged the socioeconomic activities in the SKBo region. The port of Abidjan was largely inaccessible to inland countries for almost five years. Before the civil war broke out in Côte d'Ivoire in 2002, more than 60% of imports and exports from/to Burkina Faso, Mali, and Niger, were transited through Abidjan, representing about 7% of the total traffic handled by the Abidjan port. The Ivorian crisis drastically reduced the activities of the port of Abidjan by 43.4% (Panapress 2003). Burkina Faso and Mali had to shift from Abidjan to other big ports, such as Conakry (Guinea), Cotonou (Benin), Dakar (Senegal), Lomé (Togo), Nouakchott (Mauritania), Takoradi, and Tema (Ghana) to sustain their economies. Due to the Ivorian crisis, many immigrants came into the SKBo area (Dahou 2007 et al. 27). Therefore, the Ivorian crisis shed light on the importance of borderland regions (Dahou et al. 2007, 15).

---

the technical and financial partners. The aim is that the territorial authorities should become more capable of exercising their responsibilities. Authorities in border areas are faced with special challenges in meeting the needs of their populations: identifying a common vision for the development of a particular cross-border area; and the development of consistent and co-ordinated policies on both sides of the border (in fields such as culture, education, health, transport, economic development and land-use planning), as well as of services, infrastructure and cross-border public amenities (to avoid any duplication). In this respect, the cross-border issue has to be part and parcel of the decentralisation process" (9–10).

This crisis divided Côte d'Ivoire into the North and the South (the main part of the Ivorian economy). This division not only seriously damaged the economy in Côte d'Ivoire but also the economies of the inland countries depending considerably on transport via the port of Abidjan, such as Burkina Faso, Mali, and Niger. During the Ivorian crisis, the northern region was practically ruled by the rebel group (at that time), *La force nouvelle*, led by Soro, then-president of the National Assembly, under a militarized structure. In the northern area, the borders with neighboring countries became more important owing to this area's economic isolation from the South.

However, the civil war ironically stimulated regional trade from/to northern Côte d'Ivoire, often across the borders with Burkina Faso and Mali from/to Benin, Ghana, Guinea, Togo, and Nigeria in order to sustain the economic activities. A network of Malinke Muslims contributed to the socioeconomic activities in the isolated northern territory of Côte d'Ivoire. The Ivorian crisis made the SKBo region a newly activated economic zone fostering cultural solidarity in terms of creating a regional network. While the separation from the southern region and economic capital of Abidjan was maintained, the northern region became an epicenter of illegal trade, exporting agricultural (e.g., cocoa, cashew, cotton) and mining products (e.g., diamond) through the ports of Lome and Accra via Burkina Faso and Mali (Nassa 2008, 9–10).

During the Ivorian crisis, people were reminded of the importance of solidarity in the SKBo region. The *Kurumba* ("stepladder" in Bambara) network of radio stations was created in the SKBo region. It comprised five community radio stations, including Radio Munyu in Banfora, Kénédougou in Sikasso, Yeelen and Folona in Kadiolo, and Danaya in Zegoua (WABI 2006, 31). This involved the communities in the SKBo area in direct exchange and communication. Further, the youth in the borderlands (Mali, Burkina Faso, and Côte d'Ivoire) undertook cross-border cooperation activities (WABI 2007b, 25).

Apart from the SKBo area, Burkina Faso has other potential triangle border areas. For example, IIRSahel, shared with Niger and Mali, has been expected to promote cross-border cooperation, and the Liptako–Gourma region has broadened the borderlands between Burkina Faso, Mali, and Niger, covering an area of 370,000 km². The IIRSahel project is a program supporting agricultural development (UNCDF 2012, 13).

In particular, the borderlands in the northern regions neighboring Mali have increased the crucial meaning of security for Burkina Faso. Burkina Faso fought wars with Mali twice, in the 1970s and the 1980s (Chapter 4). Thus, its relations with Mali have been Burkina Faso's serious concern since its independence. In recent years, Burkina Faso has faced security threats from the rebel groups that have repeatedly attempted to cross the border from the Malian territory, while Mali has been suffering from the political vacuum and instability resulting from the coup d'état that occurred in 2012. In terms of this security concern, cross-border local cooperation is more critical for Burkina Faso. Therefore, it has been actively involved in local cooperation, especially cross-border cooperation.

There is an example of significant cross-border local cooperation between the local governments of Mopti (Mali) and Ouahigouya (Burkina Faso). The Dogon and Mossi communities were close neighbors throughout long precolonial history. In addition, this region was ruled by the same administrative unit of French Soudan (currently Mali) from 1932 to 1947. Therefore, this area has kept close and strong ties. In the local government cooperation, these two local governments have been keen to develop diverse cooperation through the sister-city framework and sectors such as health, agriculture, livestock, and security (WABI 2005, 12).

In 2004, the ECOWAS Cross-border Initiatives Programme (CIP) was initiated to resolve border disputes among West African countries. While border areas show potential for development, these areas are fertile grounds for conflicts, insecurity, drug and human trafficking, and arms sales. The movement of people and the trade of all kinds of products take place on both sides of the border. Therefore, cross-border cooperation is crucial for promoting socioeconomic activities in the borderlands while successfully avoiding problems. However, political instability makes it difficult to maintain cross-border cooperation. The Malian political crisis after the coup d'état made cross-border cooperation in Mali increasingly difficult, as many sites became inaccessible due to attacks and occupations by rebel forces (UNCDF 2012, 10).

Between Benin and Niger, there are historically established ties between the borderland cities of Malanville (Benin) and Gaya (Niger), located on either side of the Niger River. These two cities have constructed a community on the basis of shared languages and traditions. However, the Niger River became a demarcation between the colonial administrative unit of Dahomey (currently Benin) and Niger under the French colonial structure. The community on the Nigerien side was called Gaya, and that on the Beninese side was called Malanville, derived from the name of a French military general. The cross-border cooperation framework has great expectations for this historically fostered borderland (WABI 2004, 27).

The market of Malanville has been growing, attracting new populations and creating new jobs, owing to the price advantage it offers as compared to the bordering countries. Malanville benefits from its strategic location between the coastal and the Sahelian countries. This is the gate from/to the Sahel region that benefits from transportation via the Niger River. This area also shares a border with Nigeria. Thus, the Malanville–Gaya cross-border dynamism might provide great potential on the Nigerian side. This network is expected to involve the Nigerian city of Kamba, especially with respect to the development of the grain market (WABI 2004, 28–29, 31).

5.5. Conclusion

This chapter reflected on the border and regional security issues of Burkina Faso and its neighboring West African countries from the perspective of cross-border local cooperation. Cross-border local cooperation highlighted the challenges and potential for managing boundaries in borderlands for regional security, economic development, and integration. In the historical context, the issue of borders has been a serious national and regional security concern for African countries since their independence. African countries have faced many cases of border disputes and political destabilization due to such border-related problems.

However, border-related security concerns have changed in character in recent years and have become increasingly complicated. It has become easier for jihadist and rebel groups to cross national borders and regionalize (globalize) their activities. In Nigeria, Boko Haram announced its affiliation with the Islamic State, and in other parts of Africa, some rebel groups are affiliated with AQIM. On the one hand, a border might be a convenient membrane that allows rebel groups to defend themselves; on the other hand, a border still represents a strong sovereign wall for the national armies of African countries.

In order to promote cross-border cooperation, it is indispensable to ensure the active involvement of local governments and people inhabiting the borderlands. The decentralization process in Africa has more or less brought about the liberty of activities and the responsibility of governance for local leaders, although the devolution from the central government to the local governments is incomplete. Decentralization may not only be expected to encourage cross-border cooperation for economic development and the improvement of the lives of local residents but also to promote national and regional security. Poverty might provide a good recruitment opportunity for jihadist groups. In the context of the recent terror attacks in Burkina Faso, Côte d'Ivoire, and Mali, jihadist groups had reportedly recruited local people who perceived maltreatment on the part of the central government and were, thus, resentful. The residents of borderlands or marginalized areas might be more likely to share such resentment. In that sense, cross-border local cooperation is essential for developing the local people's lives and ensuring that they are not tempted to join in jihadist activities.

However, this chapter does not conclude that decentralization is a panacea-like measure for resolving any problems in the local communities and for promoting local development, poverty reduction, cross-border cooperation, local democracy, and security in borderlands. On the contrary, we need to consider that decentralization might create problems and disputes in local politics and governance. Therefore, we cannot expect too much from decentralization; rather, we should consider it as an important institutional option for achieving the above-mentioned objectives because the central governments and Heads of State in African countries are likely to neglect the borderlands unless the leaders come from these regions or they are resource-rich regions. Therefore, we need to highlight that decentralization is an unignorable optional measure that might contribute to the promotion of cross-border cooperation and borderland security.

The cross-border cooperation among local governments is expected to strengthen border security while uncovering the activities of rebel forces, illegal transactions or the smuggling of arms, drugs, minerals, and agricultural products, and human trafficking across borders. However, African countries have always faced limitations in their capacity for border control due to insufficient financial, human, and technical resources.

This chapter focused on Burkina Faso because this country once had a reputation as a model of decentralization and was the aggressive sponsor of local governments' international cooperation. Indeed, Ouagadougou played host to two international meetings for local cooperation (*Assises de la cooperation décentralisée*). The Malian government organized a similar international meeting in Bamako. Both Burkina Faso and Mali have a common interest in developing local cooperation to ensure national security as well as local development, especially through the cross-border local cooperation framework. However, political instability in the two countries caused serious damage to cross-border local cooperation, especially after the coup d'état in Mali in 2012 and the popular insurgency in Burkina Faso in 2014.

In Mali, the northern region has not been under the effective control of the central government, despite broad deployments of an international peacekeeping operation with France, the United States, and the United Nations after the coup d'état created a significant political power vacuum. In Burkina Faso, after President Compaoré was ousted by the insurgency of 2014, the councils of the local governments (*communes*), composed of elected mayors and councilors, were dissolved by the transitional government (Zoure 2014) to eradicate the influence of the former regime as well as the National Assembly, because the representatives of the local governments (the council of commune) were dominated by the Congress for Democracy and Progress (*Congrès pour la démocratie et le progrès*, CDP), the dominant party during the Compaoré regime. The transitional government temporarily sent governors to govern local bodies until the installation of new local representatives after the municipal elections (held in May 2016).

Since the transitional government dissolved the local governments in November 2014, international cooperation among the local governments has been practically suspended in Burkina Faso without any true local leadership or initiative. The cross-border local cooperation between Burkina Faso and neighboring countries also became inactive. Therefore, it is necessary to normalize the institution of local governance to restart cross-border local cooperation.

Chapter 6

Transforming Asia–Africa Relations: Old and New Boundaries[1]

6.1 Introduction

China hosted the third Forum of China–Africa Cooperation (FOCAC) in Beijing in 2006. Subsequently, the Chinese government boosted its cooperation with Africa and published a document titled *China's African Policy* (Iwata 2012b, 213–16). At this forum, China has declared a worldwide influential development partner with African countries from outside the established foreign aid donor community by highlighting a win–win approach in which a "developing" development cooperation provider can also seek to benefit from a development assistance project combining trade and investment. It was a major turning point not only for China–Africa relations but also for Asia–Africa relations overall. Other influential Asian partners, such as South Korea and India, followed, launching their forums for development with African countries in the late 2000s. Then African forums flourished through South–South cooperation-providing countries, such as Brazil, Indonesia, and Russia.

This chapter is intended to reflect on the transformation of Asia–Africa relations by revisiting the postcolonial history of these relations and overviewing recent phenomena in the twenty-first century.

The environment and structure of international relations have changed over time. US unipolar rule in post-Cold War world politics and economics faded in the twenty-first century after non-Western global powers (re-)emerged as influential actors in various regions (e.g., Brazil, China, India, and Russia). G7 countries are no longer the sole privileged decision-makers in the multipolar world order, although these countries still strongly influence the African continent and other parts of the world.

After Asian countries began and accelerated rapid and continuous economic growth in the 1980s, the economic gaps between Asian and African countries

---

[1] This chapter is a revised and expanded version of the article published in *Cuadernos de Nuestra America* (Centro de Investigaciones de Política Internacional [The International Policy Research Center], CIPI): Iwata, T. (2022b). Las relaciones entre Asia y Africa en el pasado y el futuro. *Cuadernos de Nuestra America*, No.6, CIPI (Cuba), 160–71. The author thanks CIPI for the permission to reproduce this work.

significantly expanded. As the economic and diplomatic power balance changed, interregional relations between Asian and African countries significantly transformed. Although the concept of solidarity remains familiar rhetoric, the Global South is no longer a homogenous and horizontal entity; rather, new boundaries have been established between and within Asian and African regions.

Hence, it is crucial and timely to rethink Asia–Africa relations to understand the transforming world order that has significantly influenced the intercontinental relations between Asia and Africa, and more dramatically so in the twenty-first century. In the multipolar era, Asia–Africa relations have become a more crucial issue in considering the new world order and multilateral cooperation.

This chapter highlights the transformation of Asian countries' approaches to African countries to reflect on Asia–Africa relations in a contemporary context. Some Asian countries have become more visible as influential development assistance partners on the African continent. It is meaningful to examine these Asian countries' engagements with Africa by creating new boundaries between Asia, Africa, and the Global South.

6.2. Historical Overviews of Postcolonial Asia–Africa Relations

6.2.1. Traditional Relations between Asia and Africa

Almost all Asian and African countries achieved independence during the Cold War period, and these newly independent countries were inevitably embroiled in West–East rivalries. Although it was very challenging for the newly independent countries to remain autonomous in the Cold War circumstances, most Asian and African countries tried to maintain neutrality. Many African countries joined the Non-Aligned Movement (NAM) with newly independent Asian countries.

The NAM had its roots in the struggles for independence in Asia and Africa and sought equality and solidarity among the Third World countries to protect their sovereignty through South–South Cooperation (SSC) (Bergamaschi et al. 2017a, 1–2). The concept of SSC not only includes humanitarian assistance but also business activities (trade and investment). The NAM provided an essential philosophy for the New International Economic Order (NIEO) (Kragelund 2019, 29).

The Asian–African Conference hosted by Indonesian President Sukarno in Bandung in 1955 initiated the quest of newly independent Asian and African leaders for solidarity to keep and foster political independence and diplomatic neutrality in the Cold War world. During the Cold War, the international solidarity between Asian and African countries was framed by the idea of the

NAM, on the initiative of Indian Prime Minister Nehru and Ghanaian President Nkrumah, with other Third World leaders. Asian and African countries principally worked together as equal partners during that period, although there were cultural, economic, political, and military gaps and varieties among the NAM member countries.

India forged close relationships with African countries after gaining its independence. Gandhi's non-violent resistance philosophy influenced African leaders (Dubey & Biswas 2016, 3), and India led the NAM with African leaders. India established its technical training program, Indian Technical and Economic Cooperation (ITEC), in 1964, which was recognized as a symbol of India's SSC, based on solidarity, national ownership, and no-conditionality (Mthembu 2018, 130; Purushothaman 2021, 163, 182–83).

(The People's Republic of) China needed Africa in order to be recognized as a genuine representative of the Chinese territory and people in the international community and to return to the United Nations (UN) in the 1950s and 1960s. Therefore, China provided maximal SSC to African countries despite its scarce financial situation and sociopolitical confusion during the Cultural Revolution period. The Tanzania–Zambia railway project (TAZARA) remains the most symbolic project in China's history of SSC in Africa (Kragelund 2019, 34).

After the Cuban revolutionary regime was established in 1959, SSC became a core approach to Africa through the NAM and revolutionary ideology, from medical to military assistance, especially during the Cold War (Benzi & Zapata 2017, 85, 100–01). Cuba hosted international meetings for Third World solidarity, such as the Tricontinental Conference in 1966 and the NAM Summit in 1979 (Benzi & Zapata 2017, 86).

SSC providers have conducted development assistance since the 1950s. SSC combines humanitarian, trade, and investment, unlike Northern donor countries, which strictly separate humanitarian aid and business. SSC has been operated with different criteria to the OECD–DAC, based on mutual benefit, no-interference, equality, and no-conditionality. Traditionally, the volume of SSC has been much smaller than that of traditional donors (Purushothaman 2021, 8). In the 1980s, South–South trade covered 3–5% of world trade. However, South–South trade began to expand in the late 1990s; from 5% in 1998, it grew to 15% in 2013 (Kragelund 2019, 32).

6.2.2. Transforming Asian Partners

Since the 1990s, the international relations environment has drastically changed, primarily due to the end of the Cold War. In addition, the economic conditions in the Global South have significantly changed, gradually revealing the expanding economic gap among Global South countries and regions. The

Global South is no longer homogeneous; the economic gap has been expanding over the years. The SSC among developing countries has rapidly expanded in volume in the twenty-first century. Now, we observe "North of South" and "South of South" among Global South countries (Purushothaman 2021, 9, 50). Emerging SSC-providing countries have played a dual role as recipients of foreign aid from Northern countries and providers of development assistance to other developing countries for decades. This has shaped the character of SSC, such as non-interference and mutual benefit-seeking (Purushothaman 2021, 220).

Now, China is the second-largest economy in the world, although it continues to consider itself a "developing" country. The nominal GDP ranking list includes, for example, India (6th), South Korea (10th), Russia (11th), Brazil (12th)[2], Mexico (15th), Indonesia (16th), and Turkey (19th) in the first twenty largest economies (World Bank 2021). On the one hand, the G20 has become one of the most powerful and comprehensive frameworks of world leadership. On the other hand, the G7, once the most influential meeting of world leaders since the 1970s, has reduced its presence in recent decades.

Global South countries became highly visible in Africa in the globalizing twenty-first century. Although China became the second largest world economy, competing against the United States, China identifies itself as a leading "developing" and SSC partner, never as a "developed" and foreign aid donor country. In the 2010s, China established the Belt and Road Initiative (BRI) and Asian Infrastructure Investment Bank (AIIB) to create its initiative for development assistance, trade, and investment. The Chinese government also announced the Global Development Initiative (GDI) at the UN General Assembly in 2021 (Center for International Knowledge on Development 2023, 1) to lead humanitarian and technical cooperation in its approach. However, in Chinese cooperation, local governments are significantly involved in SSC in addition to the central government (Kragelund 2019, 93). The Chinese government established

---

[2] Brazil also expanded its presence as the giant SSC-providing country over the years. Lula administration accelerated SSC since 2003 (Purushothaman 2021, 64). Brazil began its SSC with other developing countries (mainly Latin American and Caribbean countries) in the 1960s in a modest volume (Mawdsley 2012, 96), as well as being a foreign aid recipient (Purushothaman 2021, 64). Brazil established its SSC coordinating organization, *Agência Brasileira de Cooperação* (ABC), in 1987 (Purushothaman 2021, 75). Brazil has been keen to increase its SSC in Lusophone African countries in recent decades. However, the ABC has not centralized the Brazilian SSC under its control. Other ministries and organizations, such as the Brazilian Agricultural Research Corporation (EMBRAPA), have not necessarily worked under ABC's coordination (Kragelund 2019, 97; Purushothaman 2021, 202).

its technical and humanitarian assistance organization, the China International Development Cooperation Agency (CIDCA), in 2018 (Purushothaman 2021, 116).

India has provided modest SSC assistance since the 1950s (Purushothaman 2021, 158). India liberalized its economy (from socialist economic policy) in the early 1990s and dynamized its foreign policy (Dubey & Biswas 2016, 1). With its rapid economic growth, India expanded its presence in the Global South. The Indian government established the Development Partnership Administration (DPA) under the Ministry of External Affairs (MEA) in 2012 to coordinate its development assistance. However, other major stakeholders, such as the Ministry of Finance (MoF), including the Export-Import Bank of India, and the Ministry of Commerce and Industry (MoCI), run their assistance operations outside the DPA's control (Purushothaman 2021, 20, 183, 191).

Although Japan has been Asia's sole long-time OECD–DAC member (since the 1960s), Western members have considered Japan a "different" donor (Kragelund 2019, 9). For decades, Japan has preferred to offer loans rather than grant financial aid and to undertake infrastructure projects rather than humanitarian ones (Mawdsley 2012, 38). Japan has kept its "Asian" character in its foreign aid in the Western-based foreign aid architecture. South Korea transformed from an aid recipient and SSC-providing country to a Northern donor over seven decades. It joined the OECD in 1996 and DAC in 2010. South Korea also keeps its "Asianness" in foreign aid, for instance, by tying its foreign aid projects to Korean firms.

The combination of the rapidly expanding influence of China and India, two Asian giant leaders in the Global South, and the engagement of Asian "Northern" donors, such as Japan and South Korea, has significantly changed the landscape of Asia and African relations, especially in the twenty-first century. The concept of solidarity between the two regions remains today. However, it no longer has any deeper meaning than rhetoric. The traditional northern donors of the OECD–DAC countries can no longer neglect influential SSC providers and are keen to approach these countries (Mawdsley 2012, 179–80).

In addition to Africa's four major Asian partners (China, India, Japan, and South Korea), some other emerging Asian countries have keenly approached African countries. Indonesia is one of the most aggressive and potential ASEAN partner countries to engage with Africa. The Indonesian government hosted its first Africa forum, the Indonesia–Africa Forum (IAF), in 2018 and its first Africa business forum, the Indonesia–Africa Infrastructure Dialogue, in 2019 in Bali. Indonesian firms have aggressively invested and run their businesses in African countries over the decades. The author visited the Indomie instant noodle factory, one of Indonesia's most internationally recognized food-producing companies, which has significantly expanded its market share in Africa.

Figure 6.1 Indomie Instant Noodle Factory

Source: Author (June 2022, Bishoftu, Ethiopia)

Indonesia began to show its ambition to reach the status of a global power beyond an ASEAN leader. In addition to economic interests and energy security, Indonesia needs broad diplomatic support from the African continent to behave as a global player in international relations. The IAF became a significant milestone for Indonesia for economic and diplomatic motives. Furthermore, in 2022, the Indonesian government hosted the G20 summit and invited the African Union for the first time as the G20 chair country (Dorigné-Thomson 2022, 39–44).

6.3. A New Era of Asia–Africa Relations in the Twenty-First Century

6.3.1. Boundary between "Developed" and "Developing" Countries

The world's power (economic, military, and political) balance has drastically changed in the twenty-first century, as it has in Asia. Three decades ago, Japan was the sole prominent economic giant in Asia. Japan's (nominal) GDP size was triple compared to the sum of China, India, and South Korea in 1990 (World Bank 1990). However, in 2021, China's GDP tripled in volume compared to that of Japan (World Bank 2021). India and South Korea have also been rapidly catching up to Japan. ASEAN grew as an attractive global economic hub. This drastic change in economic circumstances in Asia has inevitably affected Asia–Africa relations.

The emerging countries have strengthened their engagement with Africa, especially since the 2010s, and this might affect the global aid structure (Owa 2020, 237–39). We have observed more cases of encounters between emerging (SSC) partners and traditional (Western, including Japan) foreign aid donor countries in Africa. This encounter between emerging partners and traditional donors happens among Asian stakeholders. Japan has been a traditional foreign aid donor as an old OECD–DAC member from Asia since the 1960s. South Korea has been a new Asian OECD–DAC member since the 2010s and has transformed from a developing aid recipient country. Despite their tremendous economic and diplomatic power, China and India are keen to keep their status as SSC providers (outside the OECD–DAC criteria) (Iwata 2012b).

The boundary between "developed" and "developing" countries was evident in the twentieth century: developed countries were foreign aid donors, and developing countries were aid recipients. Although Western countries have led the international community in foreign aid, the boundary has increasingly blurred. We have even observed some inverted situations where "developing" countries have financially supported "developed" countries, especially during the European financial crisis at the end of the 2000s. China expanded its investment in European countries.

In the current transforming and multipolar world order, the author edited the book *New Asian Approaches to Africa — Rivalries and Collaboration* (Vernon Press, Iwata 2020a) with prominent Asian scholars of African studies and African scholars of Asian studies. Asia–Africa relations have become more culturally, demographically, economically, and politically focal issues in understanding the current international relations.

Figure 6.2. New Asian Approaches to Africa (Vernon Press, 2020)

Source: Vernon Press

This book aims to provide materials and analyses for a comparative perspective by examining Asian countries' different approaches to the African continent and reflecting on the history and transformation of Asia–Africa relations. This book deliberately (unilaterally) examines the approaches of four major Asian countries—China, India, Japan, and South Korea—by highlighting their Africa forum processes, cultural approaches, business engagements, and transformation of their foreign aid structures.[3] Asia–Africa relations have been transformed by intertwining the governmental and private sectors with different objectives.

6.3.2. New Era of Asian Approaches to Africa

As the world's power balance shifted from a unipolar to a multipolar structure, the relationship between Asian and African countries significantly changed in the twenty-first century. Four major Asian countries—namely, China, India, Japan, and South Korea—became more visible and influential in Africa in the 2000s. These four countries have repeatedly hosted forums for Africa's development (Iwata 2012b, 2020a).

The influential Asian actors in development assistance in African countries differ significantly in their approaches to Africa. China and India are (non-OECD) SSC providers, whereas Japan and South Korea are OECD–DAC donor countries (Iwata 2012b). On the one hand, SSC combines humanitarian assistance and business (trade and investment). Therefore, the benefits within SSC are not likely evenly distributed among Global South stakeholders. Although concepts like solidarity and people-to-people in SSC remain relevant, they have become more rhetoric than true ideological engines (King & Venkatachalam 2021, 188). On the other hand, the OECD–DAC criteria strictly require the separation of aid and business.

In recent decades, SSC has remarkably expanded in volume. Traditional foreign aid donors can no longer neglect influential SSC in Africa and other Global South regions. Traditional Northern donors are approaching and collaborating more with SSC providers. Northern countries are more likely to

---

[3] This book is composed of three main parts. The first part rethinks the history and characteristics of Africa's development forums hosted by four major Asian countries, such as the FOCAC (Wu 2020), IAFS (Biswas 2020), KOAF (Kim 2020), and TICAD (Takahashi 2020), since the 1990s. The second part reflects on the cultural influence of Asian countries on Africa, such as South Korea's cultural approaches to Africa (Chang 2020), China's outbound tourism in Africa (Pan 2020), and Japan's soft power strategies in Africa (Iwata 2020b). The third part examines new issues in Asian approaches to Africa, such as North–South triangle cooperation between Japan–Brazil–Mozambique (Raposo 2020), Japanese firms' engagements in African markets (Cornelissen 2020), and the potential for the transformation of the foreign aid structure (Owa 2020).

adopt the concepts of win–win and mutual benefits. This trend is called the "Southernization" of development assistance (Kragelund 2019, 158). The foreign aid structure should be reconsidered as the environment of international cooperation changes (Owa 2020).

China, as the world's factory, has undertaken enormous economic development since the 1990s after the economic reform launched by President Deng. In the twenty-first century, China has become an influential economic power worldwide. China launched its Africa forum, the Forum of China–Africa Cooperation (FOCAC) (Wu 2020), in 2000. In the 2010s, China launched several new international cooperation institutions, such as the AIIB and BRI. China began to pursue its place as a new world hegemonic power. However, owing to China's slowing economic growth, it must reflect on its approach to Africa in recent years.

India initiated its Africa forum process, the India–Africa Forum Summit (IAFS) (Biswas 2020), in 2008. Among the four major Asian countries, India established a particular human network in Africa for centuries with the Indian diaspora. For the Indian government, Gandhi is the symbolic icon for bridging between India and Africa. For decades, since their independence from European rule, India and African countries have collaborated as NAM partners. However, India's approaches to Africa have become more pragmatic since its economic reform initiated in the early 1990s. India needs Africa not only for its energy supply and export but also for massive diplomatic support to reach permanent membership in the UN Security Council (Venkatachalam & King 2021, 2). India and Japan share a common interest in this ultimate diplomatic objective.

Japan launched its Africa forum, the Tokyo International Conference on African Development (TICAD) (Takahashi 2020), the first among Asian countries, in 1993. Japan enjoyed its status as the worldwide and sole Asian giant aid provider to African and other developing countries in the 1990s. However, Asia's economic and geopolitical situation drastically changed during the first two decades of the twenty-first century. Due to three decades of an economic slump, Japan is no longer the world's second-largest economy and a prominent economic giant in Asia. Although Japan remains one of the leading development donors in African countries, it will need a different approach and strategy to Africa in the future.

South Korea started its Africa forum, the Korea–Africa Forum (KOAF) (Kim 2020), in 2006. It was the ultimate diplomatic objective for South Korea to transform from a "developing" country into a "developed" aid donor country. South Korea's African policy is significantly based on this diplomatic principle. South Korea joined the OECD in 1996 and became a member of the Development Assistance Committee (OECD–DAC) in 2010 (OECD 2021). This enabled South Korea to complete its transformation from an SSC provider to an OECD (Northern) foreign aid donor. South Korea needed to host its Africa forum to step up and strengthen its international status and transform from a developing to a genuinely developed country. Once its diplomatic goal was achieved, South Korea needed to reconsider the direction of its African policy.

6.4. Transforming Relations between Asia and Africa

6.4.1. Diversification of Development Assistance Structures

As the world order has transformed, the style of development assistance has changed. In the twentieth century, bilateral cooperation between a Northern "developed" country (foreign aid donor) and a Southern "developing" country (aid recipient) was the major style of development assistance cooperation. When some aid projects ran multilaterally, this was coordinated in the international organization's framework or aid coordination led by OECD countries.

A different partnership style became more visible in the twenty-first century as the (re-)emerged SSC providers became influential.[4] SSC is not a new concept in international cooperation but has been conducted since the beginning of the postcolonial era. SSC ran in parallel with a major approach of North–South foreign aid conducted by the OECD aid donors (OECD–DAC). The international foreign aid community of the OECD–DAC member countries neglected SSC in the twentieth century in terms of its modest volume and impact on world politics and economy.

The world economic power balance has changed the foreign aid or international cooperation framework in the twenty-first century. Some influential non-OECD countries, such as Brazil, China, India, Indonesia, and Russia, have (re-)emerged as significantly influential SSC conductors in Africa. The traditional aid architecture no longer neglects SSC. The global aid architecture has been gradually shifting from the unipolar system led by the OECD–DAC members to a multipolar system (Owa 2020, 237) in which Southern actors are more involved in international cooperation, not as aid recipients but as development assistance conductors.

Emerging Global South development assistance partners are reluctant to join the OECD–DAC to sustain their free activities rather than be under the OECD aid rule. Newly emerging international cooperation-providing countries have

---

[4] South–South and triangular cooperation have no internationally recognized definition nowadays (Raposo 2020, 188). Non-OECD countries do not like to use the word "Aid" for their development assistance (Owa 2020, 240) because these countries' activities are not only concluded in "aid" but also included in business-friendly approaches.

become more influential and visible. SSC providers have spent more, whereas some OECD–DAC member countries have reduced their aid budget. As (re-)emerging SSC actors became more visible and influential in Africa, OECD aid donors began changing their approaches in recent years, likely to be more business-friendly by pursuing their national interests, by parallel pursuing the traditional humanitarian approaches to Africa. Western firms even collaborate with Chinese firms in international cooperation conducted in Africa (Owa 2020, 252). Over the years, the gap between the OECD donors and the non-OECD countries has reduced. Africa is the forefront region where foreign aid architecture is shifting, and this trend urges the transformation of the aid architecture.

India has led the NAM and the Third World since the 1950s. India had conducted its SSC with other developing countries, although its volume was modest before its economic liberalization and development, which increased its economic capacity. India established its technical cooperation program, ITEC, in 1964, earlier than other SSC providers (Purushothaman 2021, 163). As India has achieved remarkable economic development since the 1990s, the country has significantly expanded its financial cooperation with other Global South countries. Lines of Credit (LoCs) from India's Export-Import Bank (EXIM Bank) and other Indian banks represent an essential framework (King & Venkatachalam 2021, 191). India's LOCs to Africa increased from USD 304 million in 2004–05 to USD 5.1 billion in 2012–13 (Purushothaman 2021, 176). The third IAFS pledged the amount of USD 10 billion in 2015 (King & Venkatachalam 2021, 191). India's LOCs reached USD 14 billion in 42 African countries in 2021–22 (Times of India 2022). As India is not an OECD member, it does not need to respect the OECD–DAC criteria. India's LOCs require that 75% of the credit be ordered to Indian firms (King & Venkatachalam 2021, 191).

In addition to India, Brazil is keen to behave as the leader of the Global South. Traditionally, Brazil has been the leading SSC provider in Latin America. However, in the twenty-first century, Brazil became more influential as an SSC provider in Africa, especially in Lusophone countries, to display itself as a global player, beyond a regional leader. President Lula visited 27 African countries during his first administration (2003–10) (Purushothaman 2021, 88–89). Brazil has been willing to collaborate with OECD donors (French, German, Japanese, and US aid agencies) to conduct South–South Triangular Cooperation (SSTrC) in Latin America and Africa (Purushothaman 2021, 74). Brazil has played its role by bridging between SSC providers and Northern foreign aid donors. It is also eager to gain permanent membership in the UNSC by expanding its SSC (Purushothaman 2021, 100).

6.4.2. Potentials and Challenges in Triangular Cooperation between Asia and Africa

In recent years, SSC providers and Northern foreign aid donors—in other words, non-OECD and OECD countries—have sought to collaborate. Thus, the gap between the two camps has been reduced more than in previous decades. Some Asian OECD–DAC member countries, such as Japan and South Korea, traditionally have similarities to the non-OECD countries' approaches to development assistance (Owa 2020, 239). The UN expects SSTrC to be an effective option for economic growth and poverty reduction in developing countries (Raposo 2020, 181).

Prime Ministers Modi of India and Abe of Japan, the second and third-largest economies in Asia, agreed on the South (India)–North (Japan)–South (African countries) triangular cooperation platform, Asia Africa Growth Corridor (AAGC)[5] in Delhi in 2016 (Biswas 2020, 47–48). They also agreed on the importance of peace and stability in the Indian and Pacific Oceans by sharing the idea of the Free and Open Indo-Pacific (FOIP) Strategy (Vision Document 2017, 17). For both governments, the AAGC was expected to become a balancer against China's hegemony in Asia and Africa after the BRI was launched (Panda 2020, xiv).

The AAGC highlights four pillars of its development assistance: Quality Infrastructure, Institutional Connectivity, Enhancing Capacities and Skills, and People-to-People Partnership (Vision Document 2017, 1). India expected Japan's capital capacity and high technology through collaboration in a triangular cooperation framework (Mukherjee 2021, 252).

India and Japan share a common motive in their approaches to Africa. Both countries have been keen to reform the UNSC to gain permanent membership status, and they submitted a UNSC reform proposal with Brazil and Germany (G4 group) to the UN General Assembly in 2005. However, this G4 attempt failed because of the strong opposition from China and other regional rival countries, such as Argentina, Italy, Pakistan, and South Korea. The G4 did not receive massive support from Africa at the UN General Assembly. 54 African countries' support is crucial for India and Japan to achieve their ultimate diplomatic goal. Although the G4 failed in its attempt to obtain UNSC permanent membership, this experience showed that emerging powers are

---

[5] The AAGC was elaborated by an Indian public thinktank, Research and Information System for Developing Countries (RIS, Ministry of External Affairs), and a Japanese public thinktank, the Institute of Development Economy (IDE, Ministry of Economy, Trade, and Industry) (*A Vision Document: Asia Africa Growth Corridor* 2017).

playing an increasingly crucial role in international politics (Purushothaman 2021, 100–01).

However, the AAGC remains inactive and nominal without having produced any remarkable achievements as a triangular cooperation framework since its establishment (Biswas 2022). Since the launch of its Vision Document (2017), the AAGC has not been visible diplomatically. The AAGC has not even been mentioned in the events on Africa's development hosted by either country, such as Modi's state visit to Uganda in 2018 and the 7th TICAD in 2019 (Sarkar & Panda 2021, 48). Instead, in 2018, the Japanese and Indian prime ministers welcomed discussions for a different triangular framework, Platform for Japan–India Business Cooperation in Asia–Africa Region, by the Japan External Trade Organization (JETRO) and the Confederation of Indian Industry (CII), signed in December 2019 (JETRO & CII 2019, 48). Practically, this framework remodeled the AAGC (Sarkar & Panda 2021, 48; Venkatachalam & King 2021, 17).

As emerging SSC providers are gaining visibility, triangular cooperation with influential SSC providers is becoming more attractive for traditional Northern donors. The ProSavana project was announced in 2009 and highlighted at the 5th TICAD by the Japanese government as a triangular cooperation framework with great potential. In Mozambique, agriculture has been the priority sector for cooperation. The ProSavana project aims to improve agricultural productivity in Mozambique (Kragelund 2019, 151; MASA 2015). This project was co-organized by the Japanese (Japan International Cooperation Agency, JICA), the Brazilian Cooperation Agency (*Agência Brasileira Cooperação*, ABC), and the Mozambican Ministry of Agriculture (Raposo 2020, 194).

Japan once conducted a successful aid project for *Cerrado* agricultural development in Brazil in the 1970s, and the Japanese and Brazilian governments were keen to transfer their successful experience to Mozambique (Raposo 2020, 182, 187). ProSavana aimed to make Northern Mozambique (Nacala Corridor) a highly productive agricultural area (Duran & Chichara 2017, 272). The Mozambican government had to collect huge plantation lands spanning 14.5 million hectares (Raposo 2020, 193) from small farmers who traditionally cultivated this targeted area for the ProSavana project.

However, this project faced strong protests from local farmers, who were excluded from the decision-making in the ProSavana project (Raposo 2020, 185). Small farmers complained about a lack of information disclosure on the project from the Mozambican government regarding land acquisition and financial compensation. Japanese, Brazilian, and Mozambican NGOs joined the protesting farmers and required the three government organizations—especially the Japanese aid agency, the main organizer of this project—to satisfy the small farmers' requests and interests (Raposo 2020, 195–99). Triangular civil society also condemned the remodeling of *Cerrado* in a different location and time and its negative impacts on small farmers regarding land tenure and environmental concerns (Duran & Chichara 2017, 291).

Owing to the deep involvement of Japanese and Brazilian agriculture institutes (EMBRAPA)[6] and mining (Vale)[7] and trade (Mitsui & Co.)[8] firms, this project has been guided by more commercial motives outside the Japanese aid agency's control (Raposo 2020, 182–83, 190–92, 200). Although the Japanese aid agency tried to persuade the protesters by hosting meetings, they did not reach an agreement. Eventually, the Japanese government officially announced the end of this program in July 2020 without any result for the massive agricultural products. It was a bitter experience of triangular North–South–South cooperation for the Japanese government.

When other Global South actors propose triangular cooperation with Northern partners and African countries (Fabelo Conception & Gonzalez 2020), how do these Southern countries refer to the India–Japan–Africa and Brazil–Japan–Africa cases?

Cuba was a prominent SSC provider in Africa during the Cold War. However, the disintegration of the Soviet Union resulted in Cuba losing its most crucial supporter and market (Fabelo Concepciòn 2022, 2), and then Cuba faced severe economic difficulties in the 1990s. Cuba had to adopt a more collaborative approach in its SSC. Cuba has conducted SSTrC not only with Global South but also with Global North countries, such as Turkey and Luxembourg (Fabelo Concepciòn 2022, 9). Cuba seeks other partners in its triangular cooperation framework. Japan is a potential partner for Cuba. Cuba and Japan have not engaged much in triangular cooperation in Global South countries. Japan has been more active in SSTrC in Africa and South Asia in recent decades. Cuba expects to collaborate with Japan to coordinate the SSTrC program, combining Cuba's experience, Global South-friendly technology, human resources, and Japan's financial resources (Fabelo Concepciòn 2022, 16–18).

6.5. Conclusion

This chapter examined Asia's engagement with Africa to reflect on the transforming Asia–Africa relations by revisiting the history of these relations from the postcolonial and Cold War eras to the current multipolar time. Asian

---

[6] Brazilian Agricultural Research Corporation (Brazilian Ministry of Agriculture, Livestock, and Food Supply, Empresa Brasileira de Pesquisa Agropecuária, EMBRAPA). https://www.embrapa.br/en/international (accessed February 28, 2022)

[7] Vale. http://www.vale.com/EN/aboutvale/Pages/default.aspx (accessed February 28, 2022)

[8] Mitsui & Co. https://www.mitsui.com/jp/en/index.html (accessed February 28, 2022)

and African regions have dramatically developed and expanded their economic and diplomatic relations in the twenty-first century.

The COVID-19 pandemic temporarily slowed down the expansion of Asia–Africa relations with reductions in people, goods, and financial exchange between the two regions. However, as global economic activities began normalizing, the exchange between the two regions was reanimated.

The boundaries between the Global North and the Global South and foreign aid donors and recipients became blurred over the years (Mthembu 2018, 18; Purushothaman 2021, 224) as the economic gap between Global North countries and emerging Global South countries significantly reduced. International relations in the Global South became much more complex, with significantly larger gaps than in the twentieth century (Bergamaschi et al. 2017b, 255). We find significant gaps between "North of South" and "South of South" in the Global South (Purushothaman 2021, 50). Therefore, the Global South's leading role in development assistance becomes more visible, accompanying specific challenges.

Asian countries have repeatedly hosted African development forums in the twenty-first century. SSC is a combination of development assistance and business. It derives not from a charitable philosophy but a mutual interest-seeking approach as aid recipient countries over the decades. SSC-providing countries can pursue their own interests through their development assistance projects. It is definitely a different approach from the OECD-based foreign aid philosophy. However, with time, some Global North countries partially began adopting SSC-like approaches (Southernization of foreign aid).

Traditional donor countries are also trying to regain their initiative for the post-COVID era. The G7 summit (June 2022) announced the Partnership for Global Infrastructure and Investment (a deal totaling USD 600 billion by 2025) (White House 2022) as a counter initiative against Chinese initiatives, such as the AIIB and BRI. Northern donors are also trying to attract leading SSC providers to collaborate on development assistance.

While the old boundary between the Global North and the influential Global South became blurred, the new boundary within the Global South has been distinct and significant. The relationships between Asian and African countries have changed significantly over the years. The concept of solidarity remains rhetorical and is no longer a practical engine for co-working. The world has become more multipolar and multilateral. Therefore, Asia–Africa relations remain an essential topic in reflecting on the new world order.

Chapter 7

Laughter as a Political Communication Intermediary in Africa: Boundary between Laughing and Being Laughed at[1]

7.1 Introduction

This chapter is intended to examine and reflect on laughter as a political communication intermediary in African countries. How does laughter mirror the political situation? Does laughter have potential and significance as a means of political communication? Laughter and laughter-making acts accompany everyone, from formal political scenes to the private everyday lives of ordinary people. This chapter examines how political satire is produced in (non-professional) people's daily lives and in professional comedy activities by tying laughter to politically stimulated motives that mirror the political situation in African countries.

In general, scholars studying African politics are inclined to highlight tragic or sensational aspects perceived by the so-called international community (practically, the Western world), such as authoritarianism (or failed democratization), conflict, corruption, dictatorship, failed state, human rights abuse, humanitarian crisis, or poverty. However, such politically made tragedies do not comprehensively encapsulate the lives of Africans; despite repeatedly suffering from human-made (political) disasters, African people also enjoy laughter in their everyday lives. It is a natural aspect of human life. In addition, seemingly powerless African people do not forgo laughing off, mocking, or caricaturing political leaders (e.g., dictators or beloved leaders) in their satirical humor, which changes in character according to the timing, technology, and political situation. African societies are dynamic and full of politically inspired laughter. This chapter focuses on the symbolic potential of (politically) powerless actors' behavior in African countries. In other words, it

---

[1] This chapter is a revised and updated version of the following article: Iwata, T. (2020c). Political satire and laughter in Africa. In Ofusu-Kusi, Y., & Matsuda, M. (Eds.). *The Challenge of African Potentials — Conviviality, Informality and Futurity*. Bamenda: Langaa, 143–68. The author sincerely appreciates the permission granted by Langaa Publishers for the reproduction of this chapter.

examines the political challenges that can arise from below by highlighting the political satire and laughter in ordinary people's daily activities.

Laughter is a very complicated human act. However, it is also attractive for developing a comprehensive understanding of the current situation and transformation in African politics and society. This chapter examines political satire targeting African heads of state to gain insight into how laughter mirrors the political realities and the people's reactions to authoritarian regimes.

Often, African politics is characterized by authoritarian regimes in which political leaders maintain tight control over political power and economic resources. Under such highly personalized rules, the head of state might be identified as the state itself. Therefore, the gap between powerful political leaders and powerless, marginalized people often seems huge in many African countries and societies. In such political circumstances, political satire has a crucial role to play. *Le politique par le bas* (the political thing from below, hereinafter PPB; Bayart 1981; 1992) inspires laughter in people oppressed by the state (or local) authority.

On the one hand, powerful political leaders use laughter to diminish their opponents' symbolic power and influence by laughing them off in public spaces. We usually observe a significant material and psychological boundary between the ruling and ruled actors in African countries and elsewhere. On the other hand, laughter-making acts practiced daily by ordinary and (politically) powerless people undermine the symbolic power of the political authority in African countries. Laughter-related acts from below occasionally undermine the symbolic power that authoritarian leaders in Africa have elaborated over the years and decades. Laughter might be occasionally recognized or operate as an ephemeral inverter in political power relations. Thus, laughter (or humor) can bring about a different way of thinking about political power among people.

Laughter does not directly bring about a change of political regime or leadership. However, we should not neglect its potentiality as a political communication intermediary, reducing (or temporarily inverting) the symbolic and psychological gap between politically powerful figures and powerless actors.

This chapter highlights the feeling of superiority that generates momentum for an ephemeral inversion of the symbolic power boundary between powerful and powerless actors through political satire, which is principally practiced outside the political society. The chapter examines two styles of political satire that have taken shape in recent years. The first style is personally (or non-professionally) produced political satire, and the second is professionally elaborated political satire. Regarding the first style, this chapter examines the hashtag (#[name]Challenge) movements that have spread widely on social media (e.g., #BidoungChallenge, #UhuruChallenge) and directly undermined the image and symbolic power of various African heads of state. Concerning the second style, this chapter examines political satire performed as part of various comedy activities, such as *La République très très démocratique du Gondwana* (*The Very Very Democratic Republic of Gondwana*), which intentionally caricatures a fictional dictatorial state located somewhere on the African continent.

7.2. Political Satire and Laughter

Laughter is satanic. So, it is deeply human. It is the consequence of the idea of one's superiority. Indeed, as laughter is essentially human, it is essentially contradictory… (Baudelaire 1855, 20)

This part of the chapter briefly reflects on the concept of laughter before delving into political satire, focusing on the concept of political satire as a laughter-making act in a political context and everyday life.

Laughter is omnipresent in human life and is a highly complicated human act that has no simple definition. As Bergson states, it is pretty challenging to define laughter in a comprehensive and unique way.[2] Broadly speaking, laughter extends from daily life into politics or official life, which brings not only joy but also discrimination. Laughter accompanies a broad range of human emotions, such as joy, affection, amusement, good humor, surprise, nervousness, sadness, fear, shame, aggression, victory, taunt, and *schadenfreude* (pleasure brought about by another person's misfortune) (Schaeffer 2011, 25–26). However, this chapter focuses specifically on laughter relating to a political issue to help understand how laughter mirrors political realities and offers political potential in African countries.

Morreall examines the process of laughter-making by focusing on three traditional theories regarding superiority, relief, and incongruity. According to the superiority theory, people laugh because they have a feeling of superiority over other individuals or groups. The relief theory posits that laughter is an expression of release from a very tense situation. Finally, the incongruity theory considers the gap between what was expected and what happens that produces laughter (Morreall 1987, 5–6).[3]

---

[2] Bergson (1940, 1) states, "The greatest thinkers, since Aristotle, have tackled this tiny problem which always eludes all effort and slips, escapes, and readdresses impertinent challenges to philosophical speculation."

[3] Morreall points out that these theories might not comprehensively explain all phenomena relating to laughter. However, he agrees that each theory explains an essential part of laughter (Morreall 1987, 133; Iwata 2016b, 137).

Laughter creates a certain space of psychological comfort. According to the French poet and drama writer Baudelaire (1855, 16, 20), a feeling of superiority induces laughter. This feeling of superiority also allows an individual or group to feel comfortable by looking down on others. If politics is recognized as a game in which the goal is to achieve superiority, laughter would appear to be a product of political activities (Iwata 2016b, 136). Therefore, this chapter highlights the superiority theory as a meaningful concept for better understanding laughter in African politics, although it is imperfect, as Morreall points out.

In keeping with the superiority theory, political satire (parody) can be considered an intentional act, even if produced accidentally, accompanied by laughter (but not necessarily all the time), and intended to arouse a feeling of superiority in the audience over the targeted actors. In such cases, political satire constitutes involvement in a symbolic struggle for/against perceived superiority in the political field or an ephemeral escape from political power. Besides using such political satire to generate a feeling of superiority, people deploy it to achieve ephemeral freedom from the targeted, powerful political actors (perpetrators).

Political satire can also be considered an act of PPB, which is based on the daily activities of ordinary (not politically strong) people involving laughter. The meaning of *le politique* (the political thing) is not necessarily confined to political activities carried out in political society but can also include some politics-related acts played out among non-professional political actors. Thus, the concept of PPB in this chapter means politics-inspired acts that are practiced and repeated among ordinary people outside of conventional political society.

Although political satire is not usually powerful enough, in material terms, to change the political situation directly, it might be able to gradually influence political circumstances that are based on the symbolic and psychological relationships found in everyday activities. Further, political satire may temporarily undermine the symbolic power of rulers. If nothing else, it may bring about an ephemeral and intentional inversion of the targeted authoritarian regime at a critical moment.

7.3. Political Satire in Africa

The prevailing political situation and environment inevitably affect the character and trends of political satire. In other words, political satire mirrors the political situation in a meaningful way. This is especially true in authoritarian regimes, as opposed to democratized or democratizing countries, because the freedom of expression regarding political matters in public is severely limited under an authoritarian regime. In such circumstances, ordinary people are eager to consume political satire because they have few other means of expression. Under an especially authoritarian regime, where ordinary people and media cannot directly criticize political leaders in power, political satire is likely to be expressed indirectly and anonymously to protect the political satire creators.

PPB is a research approach in the study of African politics that attracted much attention in France in the 1980s. At that time, various authoritarian regimes were flourishing throughout the continent, and this research approach was developed to understand ordinary people's political (re-)actions as practiced underground or outside of the political society in a most indirect way. This approach highlights the daily activities of politically powerless actors who enjoy political satire and laughter but who do not necessarily have justice as their first objective. Whether such acts of politics from below are deliberately practiced or not, they may still undermine the symbolic power of an authoritarian regime. This research approach refers to Bourdieu's (2001) concepts of symbolic capital and struggle.[4] Therefore, in PPB, political satire is accompanied by derision or mockery as metaphoric acts under an oppressive regime.

In any authoritarian regime, actions involving political satire targeting political leaders carry the risk of being accused of defamation. Political satire makers (whether deliberately or not) must be cautious to avoid a charge of defamation against the national leader because, as stated above, the head of state is likely to be identified as the state itself — as in "*L'Etat c'est moi*" (Louis XIV) — in such a highly personalized authoritarian state system. Thus, laughter might be used to challenge political rulers in the symbolic realm, but only while being careful to avoid the accusation of defamation. Under an oppressive political regime, political satire should, therefore, be practiced in the manner of PPB. Defamation is always the number one enemy for comedians or political satire makers operating under an authoritarian regime.

Under an authoritarian (one-party or military) regime or after the failure of the democratization process, the head of state inevitably becomes the most prominent target of political satire because the political power is concentrated in the leader's hands. However, laughter is not only a symbolic weapon for practicing PPB; it can also be used as a weapon by the political leader in power

---

[4] Bourdieu (2001, 210) describes symbolic power as "the power of constitutes the given by the enunciation, to make see and to make believe, to confirm or to transform the vision of the world and, consequently, the action on the world, thus the world, to provide quasi-magic that allows obtaining the equivalent of what is obtained by force (physical or economic), thanks to the specific effect of mobilization, is exerted only if it is recognized, that is to say, unknown as arbitrary."

to kill political opponents and potential challengers symbolically. Political opponents can be laughed off in public by the authority to emasculate them politically. Under such an authoritarian regime, PPB must be practiced indirectly, challenging the powerful ruler(s) with derision.

Toulabor has closely examined PPB-related acts practiced during the 1980s and 1990s in Togo, where politically powerless ordinary people launched counterattacks against the authoritarian political system by mocking and caricaturing their dictator in an indirect and derisive way. Toulabor explains how these PPB counterattacks used the mockery of General Eyadéma as a sexual monster and feces in various metaphors (Toulabor 1986; 1991; 1992a; 1992b). Despite the repeated symbolic counterattacks, Eyadéma maintained his powerful and immortal image (Toulabor 1993) even after sustaining damage due to the democratic transition initiated by the Sovereign National Conference in 1991 (Iwata 2000; 2004). After these democratization trials were undermined in the mid-1990s, a degree of fatalism took root in the Togolese people (Toulabor 1996). Their last hope was to await Eyadéma's death.

Despite the elaborate images of an immortal General Eyadéma built up over a decade, he eventually died in February 2005 after a long struggle with throat cancer. However, his death did not mark the end of the Eyadéma family's rule. The rule of Togo was desperately succeeded from father to son, Faure Gnassingbé, in a process marked by procedural irregularities. Owing to the failure or undermining of democratization, the Togolese people could not expect the full liberalization of laughter. Under continuous political oppression, political satire has always been meaningful in Togo. Although it is still highly challenging to mock authority directly under President Gnassingbé, there is some room for the liberalization of laughter in politics. Therefore, political satire no longer needs to be practiced underground compared to the time of his father's rule.

For instance, people may say aloud, 'Gnass did something wrong or funny.' While the word "Gnass" implies that they are talking about President Gnassingbé, this still allows some room to escape the accusation of defamation because there are some other similar (officialized) traditional family names derived from the *authenticité* policy (officially introduced in the 1970s by General Eyadéma), such as Gnassengbé (interview with an anonymous person in Togo). This example significantly reflects the currently limited degree of liberalization of laughter in Togo brought about by the failure of democratization.

Laughter vividly mirrors the actual situation in society and politics. A turnover of the political regime would significantly affect the environment for laughter. Likewise, when democratization progresses, political satire and politically elaborated laughter would also change character. In a democratized or democratizing country, politically made laughter no longer occurs underground. In other words, democratization significantly liberates political satire and laughter.

Burkina Faso offers a good example for reflecting on the correlation between the political situation and laughter because this country launched its own democratization process. President Compaoré was recognized as one of the longest-serving and most authoritarian African leaders when he was in power. He took power through a military coup d'état involving the assassination of then-President Sankara in 1987. Compaoré remained in power for 27 years, ruling in a very authoritarian style and maintaining good, close relations with France, Burkina Faso's former colonial master. This was in marked contrast to his predecessor, whose opposition to France frequently created tensions. Therefore, France found in Compaoré a convenient African leader in protecting its interests. However, after 27 years, his regime was confronted in October 2014 by massive protest demonstrations against the modification of the Constitution to allow him to carry on his presidency for life (Iwata 2016b). These protests culminated in Compaoré being practically ousted by the army, and he had to escape to Côte d'Ivoire under the French army's escort. How did this unexpected regime change influence laughter in Burkina Faso?

Figure 7.1. Son Excellence (His Excellency) Gérard

Source: Author (Radio Oméga, Ouagadougou, Burkina Faso, March 2017)

To consider this question, this section focuses on the performances of Son Excellence (His Excellency), one of the most famous comedians in Burkina Faso, who is especially renowned for his impersonation of President Compaoré in his early career. It is quite natural for African comedians to prefer to include powerful personalities, such as a military leader or especially a head of state, in their material because every audience knows them as the greatest common concern in the country. However, comedians must be extremely cautious of the risk of being charged with defamation by the state authority.

After the successful insurgency culminating in the regime turnover of 2014, "acheke" (*attiéké*) became an icon of regime change, bringing laughter to the Burkinabe people. Here, the author introduces a radio chronicle program called *La pause toilette de Gérard*, produced by Son Excellence Gérard (Ouédraogo). In March 2015, Radio Oméga broadcasted a sketch of *La pause toilettes de Gérard* in which the former President, "Blaise Kodjo," won an acheke-eating competition. Acheke is a staple food, similar to couscous, made of cassava, which is popular among Ivorians but is not so common and familiar to Burkinabe, especially to Mossi people, including the former President himself. In this particular sketch, he received Ivorian nationality as the prize for becoming champion in the acheke-eating competition. In reality, Former President Compaoré obtained Ivorian nationality to avoid prosecution in Burkina Faso for criminal acts committed during his presidency. In this sketch, acheke eloquently talks about the former president's life in exile with a satirical connotation. Mr Ouédraogo then continues to imitate the former president, making new arrangements.

7.4. Heads of State as Targets of Political Satire

This section examines examples of political satire targeting authoritarian African heads of state. As democratization processes in Africa continue to progress, the military presence is gradually becoming less visible, even on the comedy scene. In comedians' stage names, military titles, such as "Colonel," "General," and "Sergeant," are becoming less common as the military influence on politics decreases in African countries. The visibility of military personalities in terms of laughter-making or comedy significantly mirrors the political situation in a country, especially when it is still in the pre-democratization era. In other words, the visibility of the military on the comedy scene acts as a barometer (but not necessarily in all cases) of the political conditions in the democratization process. However, military actors neither matter nor attract people's attention in terms of the laughter-making process in African countries once the democratic system and values are successfully consolidated.

This section discusses two different types of political satire targeting African heads of state: political satire that is non-professionally produced in the daily lives of ordinary citizens and political satire that is deliberately produced by professional comedians. The hashtags #[name]Challenge, which have been especially popular on social media in recent years, collectively provide an excellent example of non-professionally created political satire targeting and mocking African heads of state.

7.4.1. #Challenges on Social Media

First, this subsection examines the common political satire that people encounter in their daily lives, but that is not necessarily professionally made. People live with laughter deliberately or unintentionally brought about by political satire that caricatures or mocks politically powerful (wo-)men in African countries. Political satire creators do not necessarily aim to attack political leaders and their regimes. Instead, they create political satire by targeting the head of state and other politically strong figures with a fancy (not elaborate) idea, allowing people to enjoy ephemeral relaxation and experience an inversion of the feeling of superiority in their daily lives. Although they do not necessarily intend to attack an authoritarian regime, their acts might occasionally and gradually undermine the symbolic power of the regime, which may have been elaborately established and built up over years and even decades, leading people to fear the regime and not oppose it.

With the advent of social media, it has become much easier for everyone to play PPB. Thus, if an example of eye-catching political satire accompanying an impressive picture is posted, it is likely to be shared and spread so rapidly and widely that it can easily extend beyond sovereign borders.

Figure 7.2. #BidoungChallenge greeting style reproduced by the author

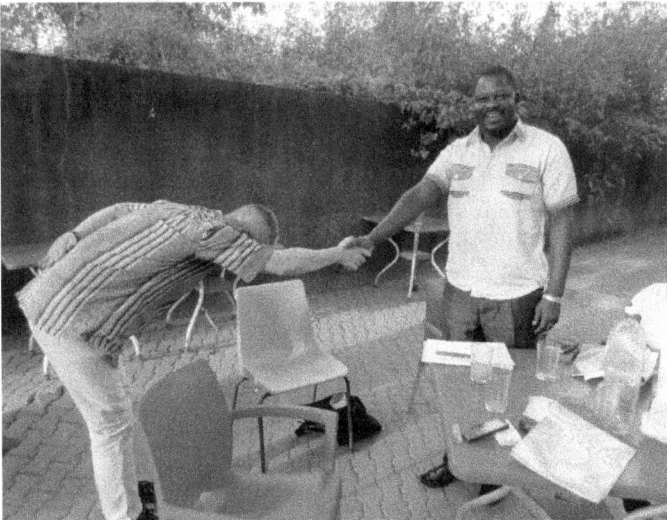

Source: Author (Ouagadougou, Burkina Faso, February 2017)

The hashtag #BidoungChallenge is an excellent example of this form of political satire from below (non-professionally made and spread). It all started when a picture of Sports Minister Bidoung Kpwatt flattering President Biya of Cameroon was posted on social media on December 10, 2016, and then went viral. He made an incredibly deep bow to President Biya while keeping a distance of a couple of meters from him — a gesture evincing fear rather than respect. That picture eloquently illustrates how much Cameroonian politicians (or African politicians in a broader sense) fear their patron.

This clearly exposed the reality of political relationships in much of Africa. After the hashtag (an index function on social media) was added, the #BidoungChallenge movement went viral and rapidly spread internationally within a week, accompanied by innumerable new versions added by social media users. People posted their own pictures of #BidoungChallenge performing the role of their Sports Minister, flattering a fictional patron in innumerable arrangements. In addition, a politically and socially engaging Cameroonian rapper, One Love, reacted very quickly by launching a new song on YouTube titled "Bidoung Kpwatt,"[5] and it was watched by tens of thousands of people around the world. Thus, #BidoungChallenge has been one of the most viral and influential worldwide movements related to online political satire to come out of Africa in recent years.

We can find other examples of similar online #Challenges, such as #UhuruChallenge, which mocked the Kenyan president's eagerness to take part in his ribbon-cutting (inauguration) ceremonies to maximize his presence and exaggerate his achievements in public because of the approaching presidential election (for his re-election).

In January 2017, Kenyans began posting many creative ribbon-cutting pictures of their own on social media to mock their president. This social media movement attracted international media attention. Al Jazeera summarised the movement on its Facebook page.[6] The #UhuruChallenge targeting the Kenyan president later resurfaced after his re-election in November 2017 under the new name of #InaugurationChallenge. Immediately after President Kenyatta's swearing-in ceremony for his second term, a massive number of Kenyan people, including children, posted images of their own swearing-in ceremony on social media.

Several months after the #BidoungChallenge, another hashtag, #Mama FoudaChallenge, emerged in Cameroon, targeting Public Health Minister Mama Fouda, exposing his displeased facial expressions during negotiations with doctors who were striking for better working conditions. Thus, African

---

[5] One Love, "Bidoung Kpwatt," posted on YouTube (December 16, 2016), https://www.youtube.com/watch?v=AwK5kmlzfDM (accessed December 20, 2016).

[6] Al Jazeera English Facebook page (January 10, 2017), "#UhuruChallenge takes Twitter by storm," https://www.facebook.com/aljazeera/videos/10155087713453690 (accessed March 1, 2019).

#Challenges became an online *"radio trottoir"* (rumor) in the age of social media, easily crossing borders between communities and sovereign states.

7.4.2.République Très Très Démocratique du Gondwana

This subsection examines the case of professionally produced political satire. Creating political satire that directly targets a specific head of state is a very risky undertaking, especially when living under an authoritarian regime. One means of doing this is to mock and caricature the head of state and political regime by making up funny stories in a fictional country to raise consciousness about political realities while avoiding any unnecessary risk of being accused of defaming a specific African leader.

La République très très démocratique du Gondwana (The Very Very Democratic Republic of Gondwana, hereafter the "Republic of Gondwana") became an international platform for African comedy, especially in Francophone African countries[7] after its creation in 2009. A comedian from Niger, Mamane (Mohamed Mustapha), started his radio chronicle program of political satire, *"Chronique de Mamane"* (Chronicle of Mamane), on Radio France Internationale in January 2009. His program became immensely popular, gaining 30 million listeners, mainly in African countries, and his fictional Republic spread from radio to other media.

In 2012, Mamane and a French producer (Catherine Guérin) established a specialized African comedy production company, Gondwana City Productions, to institutionalize and expand the "Republic of Comedy." The Republic of Gondwana was created as a fictional country "existing somewhere" on the African continent. This parody Republic allows audiences and listeners in/from African countries to rethink their own national leaders and current political situations.

Then, the Republic of Gondwana, or Gondwana City Productions, expanded its activities from radio to include theatre, TV, social media, YouTube, and film. Gondwana City Productions, which established its headquarters in Abidjan, the commercial capital of Côte d'Ivoire, has produced stage performance events (one-[wo]man shows, duos, and comedy theatre) in various African countries, France, and neighboring European countries.

---

[7] Outside francophone countries, *What's Up Africa* was known as a political satire program broadcasted on the BBC. This video program is produced by Nigerian-British comedian Ikenna Azuike. A high wall seems to exist between the African comedians of English- and French-speaking countries.

Figure 7.3. Mamane, founder of the Republic of Gondwana

Source: Author (Abidjan, Côte d'Ivoire, February 2024)

The TV program *Le Parlement du Rire* (Parliament of Laughter) seasonally broadcasts on the French cable TV channel, Canal+. Gondwana City Productions operates *le Parlement du Rire* as an international platform to bring together a variety of francophone African comedians.

Figure 7.4. Seasonal TV programme *le Parlement du Rire* on Canal+

Source: Facebook page of *le Parlement du Rire*
(Courtesy of Gondwana City Productions)

The show regularly features the president of the parliament (Mamane) and three vice presidents (Michel Gohou, Digbeu Cravate, and Charlotte Ntamack) acting as the hosts. These hosts then invite African comedians to act as honorable parliamentarians and present their stand-up performances before an audience. The program provides opportunities for young African comedians to gain international exposure and facilitates exchanges with comedians from other African countries.

The Republic of Gondwana (City Productions) established its first regular comedy hall in Abidjan (inside Hotel Pullman) in March 2019 to foster African comedic talent by providing young comedians with opportunities to perform in front of a small audience.[8] The organization of such a regular stage for comedy is very rare in African countries. Gondwana City Productions is developing its activities as an international platform for African comedy.

In 2017, Gondwana City Productions produced a film, *Bienvenue au Gondwana* (Welcome to Gondwana), depicting the presidential election, a huge political festival held in the fictional Republic of Gondwana as the prototypical authoritarian African country.

Figure 7.5. Film Bienvenue au Gondwana

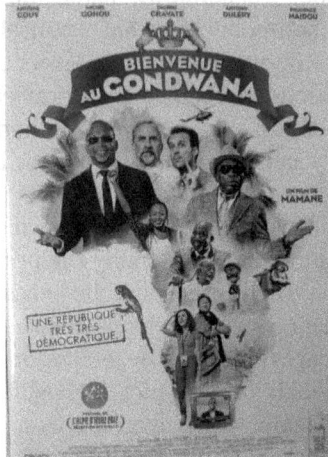

Source: DVD of Bienvenue au Gondwana

This film caricatures how elections regularly take place in African countries and how election observers are dispatched by the international community (e.g., Western countries). The film concludes by showing how the dictatorship of this fictional African country deliberately manipulates and fixes the election results in advance. Electoral observers are dispatched by the international

---

[8] Press Conference broadcasted on the Facebook page of République du Gondwana (@RepubliqueduGondwana, February 28, 2019), https://www.facebook.com/Republique DuGondwana/videos/426684704738494 (accessed March 3, 2019).

community to promote their own interests before their official mission. The people are exhausted but still have some hope.

Interestingly, a Burkinabe newspaper mentioned the Republic of Gondwana in the context of the presidential election in Russia (March 2018) and noted the similarities to Gondwana (Le Pays 2018). According to this Burkinabe newspaper, President Putin was re-elected, systematically excluding the potential opposition candidates and allowing non-threatening candidates. In general, in an authoritarian country, the incumbent president can mobilize massive state resources, in contrast to those available to the opposition candidates, for their re-election campaign. The result of the election was fixed before the polling day. Therefore, the polling operation itself took place very peacefully. This is precisely what has repeatedly happened in the Republic of Gondwana.

7.5. Conclusion

This chapter reflected on political satire and laughter in Africa, which can be considered as acts of PPB (*le politique par le bas*, or the political thing from below) directed against political authority, highlighting the political potential of ordinary people or non-political actors. Political satire often involves laughter (but not necessarily every time) and mirrors the political situation of African countries. The reactions of targeted political leaders to political satire also might mirror the political situation. In an authoritarian regime, African leaders are much more scared of laughter than those in a democratic regime because the symbolic power of political leaders might be significantly undermined by laughter. Non-democratically elected leaders are likely to depend on symbolic control and fear among the people to supplement the legitimacy of their rule. Therefore, symbolic power is crucial for many authoritarian African leaders to sustain their rule. However, akin to a kaleidoscope, political satire mirrors images differently depending on the timing, culture, and political situation. Although this chapter highlighted political satire and laughter as an act of PPB mainly focused on as a weapon of powerless people, laughter works not only positively but also negatively by bringing about fake news or unnecessarily damaging the dignity of a targeted person.

Laughter triggered by political satire would gradually undermine the symbolic capital of the authoritarian leader and regime. African people are not merely passive and oppressed actors in politics but are also active and astute. Social media dynamically made Africans join the PPB in a more relaxed fashion through political satire, caricaturing and mocking their political leaders to highlight the political absurdity. Laughter might induce to undermine symbolic and psychological boundaries between politically ruling and ruled actors. Indeed, to avoid damage to their symbolic power, some African leaders have overreacted by shutting down the internet owing to their fear of being mocked on social media by ordinary people.

Although PPB-related acts, such as political satire and laughter, do not directly seek to effect a fundamental political change by itself, such as democratization, described as a political change led by civil society (Iwata 2000; 2004), PPB might gradually undermine the symbolic power of a political ruler and provide a feeling of superiority among the people, thereby reducing their fear of the ruler and enabling them to go out and protest for regime change eventually.

A political transformation would have decisive effects on the characteristics of laughter in politics and political satire. Democratization has brought about the liberalization of laughter and comedy in African countries. Failed attempts at democratization make laughter more fatalistic in character, as was the case in Togo. At the beginning of a democratic transition, political satire is likely a political challenge or expression of anger against leaders. After the democratization process has progressed, political satire would then test political tolerance and democracy. Political satire might bring an ephemeral inversion of the feeling of superiority between powerful leaders and powerless citizens in a symbolic sense. Even if it does not reach real political inversion in the short term, it might reduce the gap in the feeling of superiority between powerful and powerless actors in the relationship of symbolic power.

This chapter principally focused on the symbolic counterattacks in African politics from below to reflect on the political potential of ordinary people. However, symbolic power could not exist without being based on material power derived from an economic, political, or military power source. Political satire and laughter in the era of social media as remarkable PPB-related activities might not change the political situation alone. However, PPB exposes unfavorable realities for political rulers and shows the potential to undermine their political dominance. It might push people to criticize and protest strong leaders and regimes. Although it is not necessarily a highly visible phenomenon in political society, it is certainly not negligible in African politics.

Conclusion:
Power and Politics in Africa:
Past, Present, and Future

This book tackled to study of *power* in African politics and international relations by revisiting its origin, definition, mechanism, and function with theoretical (conceptual) reflections and case studies. Political challenges unavoidably influence the practices of (political) power, and we must still acknowledge that power is always essential to gain a better understanding of Africa's politics. Power is not only the political engine (means) but also a goal for political actors and their supporters. Power has created, maintained, and changed boundaries in/among the political arena, societies, and states in Africa physically, symbolically, and spiritually. This book highlighted power as a human-made *boundary generator* in African politics and society. A politically made boundary creates gaps, which manifest, maintain, and change power relations while influencing people's lives. The concept of power is a classical but constantly renewed subject and goal of political study for thousands of years.

First, this book reflected on the concept of power in African politics. This book highlighted that power is an essential boundary generator in people's everyday lives, society, the political arena, and international relations. Power creates, maintains, and changes the gaps and differences in all areas of human life. Boundary-making power generates political dynamism, which accompanies asymmetrical political relations. Boundaries drawn by power in African politics are never static but are undermined, changed, modified, or erased by political engagements. Chapter 1 tackled conceptualizing (political) power and then examined issues related to power in African politics. The following chapters examined various power-related subjects, such as democratization, decentralization, border issues, cross-border (local) cooperation, Asia–Africa relations, and cultural aspects (laughter in politics) to investigate power in African countries and international relations. The intention was to clarify the conceptual meaning, mechanism, and function of power in African politics and societies after a half-century of their independence.

Democratization has been one of the most serious challenges in postcolonial African politics since its adoption at the beginning of the 1990s. With time, democratization brought about hope and disillusionment in African people. Democratization drew a blurred boundary between politically freer and authoritarian regimes among African countries and people. Although democratization is not a political reform that can be completed within one or two decades, three decades offer an appropriate timespan to reflect on its meanings, achievements, and challenges in post-colonial African politics. Chapter 2 traced the postcolonial political history and various democratization experiences in African countries. Then, this chapter classified evaluations of democratization in Africa. Although negative evaluations of democratization in Africa are dominant among political scientists, democratization significantly impacted the trend of African politics. We understood that political change without a military coup was possible after the democratization process began in Africa. For three decades, we have observed significant numbers of peaceful regime turnovers through presidential and legislative elections while simultaneously observing many cases of returns to authoritarian regimes or civil wars.

Decentralization is not only an administrative reform but also a political game changer. If devolution from the central government to local governments fully takes place, local political actors and organizations would become more politicized with increased political power and financial resources. Therefore, central governments in African countries have generally been vigilant in proceeding with decentralization-related devolution to ensure that they do not lose political control over the national territory. We must also consider politicization in decentralization in African countries in combination with their democratization process. Chapter 3 examined politicization features brought by decentralization by comparing Benin and Burkina Faso. In the globalized world, local African governments need to find new foreign partners beyond the traditional ones. Competition for local leadership became fiercer than in the pre-decentralization time. The mayor's office was transformed into a severe political battlefield to achieve political dominance. In some African countries, especially in French-speaking African countries, the mayor is not directly elected by local citizens but is co-elected among local government assembly members (*les conseillers de commune* / Councilors of basic local government). The commune assembly can discharge its mayor by a non-confidence vote of two-thirds. Decentralization might change the political boundary between the central government and local governments in African countries.

The territorial border is one of the most problematic legacies inherited from colonial master Western countries. Colonial borders or administrative unit boundaries became the sovereign national borders on the day of independence of African countries. African borders have broadly provoked many problems and conundrums in African countries and among their people. African people and states have suffered from border disputes, divisions of their living areas and compatriot groups, security issues, terrorism, and infectious diseases caused or complicated by the national borders. African borders have created numerous challenges for African people and states. However, these artificially drawn borders also have the potential to connect neighboring countries in economic, cultural, political, and security cooperation. If borders become bridges between African countries, we would see a more integrated Africa by enriching the African Continental Free Trade Area (AfCFTA) and by making continental-level security possible in the future. Chapter 4 studied border issues and disputes between Burkina Faso (Upper Volta) and Mali by tracing the history of their national borders since the French colonial time and investigating their disputes and the resolution process. Although African borders are artificial and troublesome, we cannot offer alternatives that are more realistic than the current ones. We identified some potential signs of cooperation among the borderlands of neighboring African countries.

Sovereign borders have created countless problems for African countries and people. However, African borders have the potential for socioeconomic and security development. Chapter 5 revisited the challenges and potential of African borders. Cross-border cooperation is expected to transform borders, which separate people's lives and economies, into bridges connecting people, communities, and neighboring countries, thereby strengthening regional ties and cooperation. This would enhance the continental connection and free trade. Historically, the contemporary border regions have been areas for the exchange and communication of people, goods, and cultures, such as the SKBO area, a triangle meeting area between Burkina Faso, Côte d'Ivoire, and Mali. In recent years, cross-border cooperation has increasingly been expected to prevent jihadist groups' activities in borderland regions. These radical groups have expanded their activities by crossing national borders. It is difficult for African states to resolve national security concerns with their own military and intelligence forces alone. This necessitates collaboration with neighboring countries to establish and maintain security against jihadist groups. International and local cooperation in border regions is required to carry out significant cross-border cooperation. Local governments' role in cross-border cooperation must be highlighted in addition to the national government's negotiations.

In the second half of the twentieth century, Asian and African countries were principally the partners of the Non-Aligned Movement to maintain their sovereignty from former colonial master countries and superpowers, which divided the world into two camps—namely, the capitalist and communist blocs. Solidarity was a basic philosophy in Asia–Africa relations during the Cold War. After Asian countries dramatically industrialized and developed economically in the 1990s, their relationships with African countries began to change. Chapter 6 reflected on the drastically transforming Asia–Africa relations, which have created new boundaries between the two regions. After Japan established its status as the leading donor, China, India, and South Korea became visible and influential on the African continent as emerging development assistance providers in the 2000s. China asserted its dominant presence in Africa and other Global South regions through trade, investments, development assistance, and security engagements in the 2010s. We can no longer grasp the relationship between Asia and Africa via the concept of *solidarity* owing to their significantly increasing economic, diplomatic, military, and soft power gaps. This chapter reflected on the transformation of Asia–Africa relations by tracing its postcolonial history and examining the current situation.

Politics surrounds us every day, whether we are conscious of it or not and whether we love it or not. Politics is not only generated by material relationships and struggles between people, groups, organizations, and states but also by spiritual relationships and struggles. Laughter is often a significant and influential human act in such spiritual communication in African politics, from the national political scene to people's daily actions on the streets. Chapter 7 reflected on the approach of "*le politique par le bas*" (the political thing from below) in the study of African politics. Political satire occurs in the daily practice of *le politique par le bas* by (politically less influential) ordinary people. Laughter generated by political satire does not necessarily change the political situation or regime in the short term, but in the long term, it might undermine the symbolic political power elaborately built by authoritarian rulers for years and decades. If the symbolic power built by fear is undermined through repeated laughter, one day, people will overcome their fear and begin protesting the political regime. This was partially observed in the insurgency that changed Burkina Faso's political regime in 2014. This chapter reflected on laughter as a political communication intermediary by highlighting political satire as a generator of the "political thing" (*le politique*) from ordinary people to rulers. Political satire and laughter mirror the political situation of the time, from the authoritarian regime to the political transition and democratizing regime. In the era of social media, political rulers are easily exposed by people with accompanying laughter. Politics remains common material in comedy according to the political conditions in each African country. Thus, laughter is becoming a more significant political communication intermediary.

Over the decades, power has generated, maintained, changed, and erased boundaries in African politics through political engagements (struggles). Politically generated boundaries have broadly and significantly impacted people's lives. Since African countries' independence, power has been the core interest, concern, and source of political activities and the reactions to them in African countries and societies. This book examined some limited and fragmented power-related issues to reflect on power's meanings and functions in African politics. Despite the author's three decades of dedicated research, this book's trial is far from a comprehensive understanding of power in Africa. Power was, is, and will always be the central question in African politics.

References

Africa No.1. (September 23, 2016). Bénin : vague de destitutions des maires pour "mauvaise gestion." http://www.africa1.com/spip.php?article72030 (accessed December 27, 2016).

African Arguments. (August 15, 2012). Burkina Faso: Blaise Compaoré and the Politics of Personal Enrichment.
http://africanarguments.org/2012/08/15/burkina-faso-blaise-compaore-and-the-politics-of-personal-enrichment-by-peter-dorrie (accessed February 7, 2016)

African Union Border Programme (AUBP). (2013). *Installation of a cross-border basic service infrastructure: The user's guide.* Department of Peace and Security. Commission of the African Union.

Ague, V. (July 28, 2017). Le maire de Cotonou suspendu par le ministre de la Décentralisation. Office de Radio et Télévision du Bénin (ORTB). http://ortb.bj/index.php/component/k2/item/6953-le-maire-de-cotonou-suspendu-par-le-ministre-de-la-decentralisation (accessed August 1, 2017)

Alden, C. (2007). *China in Africa.* London: Zed Books.

Auty, R. (1993). *Sustaining development in mineral economies — The resource curse thesis.* London: Routledge.

Bachrach, P., & Baratz, M. (1962). The Two Faces of Power. *American Political Science Review, 56*(4), 947–52.

Baniafouna, C. (1995). *Congo démocratie: Les déboires de l'apprentissage* (Vols. 1 and 2). Paris: Harmattan.

Banégas, R. (2003). *La démocratie à pas de caméléon — Transition et imaginaires politiques au Bénin.* Paris: Karthala.

Baudelaire, C. (1855, 2012). *De l'essence du rire.* Paris: Edition sillage.

Bayart, J-F. (1981). Le politique par le bas en Afrique Noire — Questions de Méthode. *Politique Africaine, 1,* 53–82.

———. et al. (Eds.). (1992). *Le politique par le bas en Afrique Noire.* Paris: Karthala.

———. (2006, 2nd edition). *L'État en Afrique: la politique du ventre.* Paris: Fayart.

BBC *News.* (August 6, 2000). West Africa Diamond Racket Exposed. http://news.bbc.co.uk/2/hi/africa/868338.stm (accessed February 7, 2016)

———. (January 16, 2016). Burkina Faso Attack: Foreigners Killed at Luxury Hotel. http://www.bbc.com/news/world-africa-35332792 (accessed January 17, 2016)

Benin Medias. (2016). Phénomène de destitution des maires au Bénin: L'appel de l'ANCB au gouvernement. http://beninmedias.com/news/phenomene-de-destitution-des-maires-au-benin-lappel-de-lancb-au-gouvernement (accessed December 27, 2016)

Benin To Info. (January 8, 2017). Bénin : D'un montant de 2010 milliards de FCFA, le budget général de l'Etat 2017 mis en execution. http://www.ben

into.info/2017/01/08/benin-dun-montant-de-2010milliards-de-fcfa-le-budget-general-de-letat-2017-mis-en-execution (accessed June 10, 2017)

Bénin Web TV. (September 1, 2016). Bénin : destitution en série des maires "anti-Talon." http://beninwebtv.com/2016/09/benin-destitution-serie-maires-anti-talon (accessed December 30, 2016)

Benzi, D., & Zapata, X. (2017). Good-Bye Che?: Scope, Identity, and Change on Cuba's South–South Cooperation. In Bergamaschi, I., Moore, P., & Tickner, A-B. (Eds.). *South–South Cooperation Beyond the Myths — Rising Donors, New Aid Practices?* London: Palgrave Macmillan, 79–106.

Bergamaschi, I., Moore, P., & Tickner, A-B. (Eds.) (2017a). *South–South Cooperation Beyond the Myths — Rising Donors, New Aid Practices?* London: Palgrave Macmillan.

———. (2017b). Going South to Reach North? The Case of Colombia. In Bergamaschi, I., Moore, P., & Tickner, A-B. (Eds.). *South–South Cooperation Beyond the Myths — Rising Donors, New Aid Practices?* London: Palgrave Macmillan, 245–69.

Bergson, H. (1940, 2007). *Le Rire.* Paris: Quadrige–PUF.

Biswas, A. (2020). Evolution of India–Africa Forum Summit (IAFS) Since Its Inception. In Iwata, T. (Ed.). *New Asian Approaches to Africa — Rivalries and Collaborations.* Wilmington: Vernon Press, 31–52.

Biswas, A. (April 7, 2022). Corridor in uncertainty, India and Japan must remain committed to the fruition of the Asia–Africa Growth Corridor. *The Telegraph Online.* https://www.telegraphindia.com/opinion/corridor-in-uncertainty-india-and-japan-must-remain-committed-to-the-fruition-of-the-asia-africa-growth-corridor/cid/1859423 (accessed April 7, 2022)

Le blog de la présse béninoise. (July 16, 2015). Elections communales du 28 Juin 2015 : Les résultats communiqués par la CENA.

http://pressedubenin.over-blog.com/2015/07/elections-communales-du-28-juin-2015-les-resultats-communiques-par-la-cena.html (accessed December 27, 2016)

Boétie (De La), E. (1983). *Discours de la servitude volontaire.* Paris: Flammarion.

Boko, H. (July 20, 2015). Elections communales au Bénin : Boni Yayi n'est ni mort ni enterré. *Le Monde.* http://www.lemonde.fr/afrique/article/2015/07/20/elections-communales-au-benin-boni-yayi-n-est-ni-mort-ni-enterre_4690940_3212.html (accessed December 27, 2016)

Bourdieu, P. (2001). *Langage et pouvoir symbolique.* Paris: Seuil.

Brisbane Times. (February 22, 2007). Bananas can cure AIDS: Gambian president. https://www.brisbanetimes.com.au/world/bananas-can-cure-aids-gambian-president-20070222-ge8dsx.html (accessed January 18, 2022)

Burkina24. (March 1, 2017). Burkina : Les élections municipales partielles prévues pour le 28 mai 2017. https://burkina24.com/2017/03/01/burkina-les-elections-municipales-partielles-prevues-pour-le-28-mai-2017 (accessed March 2, 2017)

———. (May 31, 2017). Municipales partielles à Bobo-Dioulasso : Le MPP se taille la part du lion à Dandé. https://burkina24.com/2017/05/31/municipales-partielles-a-bobo-dioulasso-le-mpp-se-taille-la-part-du-lion-a-dande (accessed June 7, 2017)

Center for International Knowledge on Development. (2023). *Progress Report on the Global Development Initiative 2023.*

Central Intelligence Agency. (2016). The World Factbook — Burkina Faso. https://www.cia.gov/library/publications/the-world-factbook/geos/uv.html (accessed February 24, 2016)

———. (2022). World Factbook — Cote d'Ivoire. https://www.cia.gov/the-world-factbook/countries/cote-divoire/ (accessed June 30, 2022)

———. (2022). World Factbook — The Gambia. https://www.cia.gov/the-world-factbook/countries/gambia-the/ (accessed June 30, 2022)

———. (2022). World Factbook — Niger. https://www.cia.gov/the-world-factbook/countries/niger/ (accessed June 30, 2022)

Chabal, P. (1992). *Power in Africa: An Essay in Political Interpretation.* Basingstoke: Macmillan.

———. (2009). *Africa: The Politics of Suffering and Smiling.* University of KwaZulu-Natal Press. London: Zed Books.

Chang, Y. (2020). Asia–Africa Relations — the way Korean and African cultures encounter. In Iwata, T. (Ed.). *New Asian Approaches to Africa — Rivalries and Collaborations.* Wilmington: Vernon Press, 111–34.

Cheeseman, N. (2020). Pathway to democracy. In Lynch, G., & VonDoepp, P. (Eds.). *Routledge handbook of democratization in Africa.* London: Routledge, 38–51.

Cités unies France (CUF). (2007). http://www.cites-unies-france.org (accessed December 10, 2007)

Cornelissen, S. (2020). Japanese Firms and Their Internationalization in Africa. In Iwata, T. (Ed.). *New Asian Approaches to Africa — Rivalries and Collaborations.* Wilmington: Vernon Press, 211–36.

Dahl, R. (2000). *On democracy.* New Haven: Yale University Press.

Dahou, K. et al. (2007). Le cas SKBO. In Enda Diapol. (Ed.). *Les dynamiques transfrontalières en Afrique de l'ouest.* Paris: Karthala, 15–52.

Daloz, J-P. (Ed.). (1999). *Le (non-)renouvellement des élites en Afrique subsaharienne.* Bordeaux: CEAN.

Dangnon, V. (2009). *La décentralisation au Bénin : Mémoires d'un premier quinquennat.* Cotonou: Tunde.

Diamond, L. (2009). Foreward. In Lindberg, S. (Ed.). *Democratization by elections — A new model of transition.* Baltimore: Johns Hopkins University Press, xiii–xx.

Dorigné-Thomson, C. (2022). The Attempted Extension of the Indonesian Developmental State towards Africa. *Jurnal Studi Pembangunan (Langgas), 1*(1), 38–50.

Du Bois de Gaudusson, J. et al. (Eds.). (1997). *Les Constitutions africaines publiées en langue française* (Vol. 1). Paris: Documentation Française.

———. et al. (Eds.). (1998). *Les Constitutions africaines publiées en langue française* (Vol. 2). Paris: Documentation Française.

Dubey, A-J., & Biswas, A. (2016). *India and Africa's Partnership — A Vision for a New Future.* New Delhi, New York, London: Springer.

Duran, J., & Chichara, S. (2017). Resisting South–South Cooperation? Mozambican Civil Society and Brazilian Agricultural Technical Cooperation. In Bergamaschi, I., Moore, P., & Tickner, A-B. (Eds.). *South–South Cooperation Beyond the Myths— Rising Donors, New Aid Practices?* London: Palgrave Macmillan, 271–99.

Duzor, M., & Williamson, B. (February 2, 2022). *By the numbers coups in Africa.* Voice of America. https://projects.voanews.com/african-coups/ (accessed March 26, 2022)

Eboussi Boulaga, F. (1993). *Les conférences nationales en Afrique noire: Une affaire à suivre.* Paris: Karthala.

Fabelo Concepciòn, S., & Gonzalez S-Y. (2020). Beyond Borders: International map of Cuban medical cooperation. MEMO Publishers.

Fabelo Concepciòn, S. (2022). Cooperation potentials with Cuba. Projection of Cuba–Japan triangular experiences in Sub-Saharan Africa in the education sector and capacity building. VRF Series, No.505, Tokyo: Institute of Developing Economies, 1–32.

Foreign Ministry of France. (2007). *Coopération décentralisée et développement urbain.* Government of France. http://www.diplomatie.gouv.fr/fr/article-imprim.php3?id_article=9485 (accessed on August 16, 2007)

———. (2012a). *Coopération décentralisée et développement urbain.* Government of France. http://www.diplomatie.gouv.fr/fr/enjeux-internationaux/cooperation-decentralisee/colonne-droite-21470/textes-de-reference-21678/article/definition-et-contexte-juridique (accessed October 7, 2012)

———. (2012b). *Coopération décentralisée et développement urbain.* http://www.diplomatie.gouv.fr/fr/enjeux-internationaux/cooperation-decentralisee/colonne-droite-21470/outils-et-methodes/article/cofinancements-outils-et-guide (accessed October 7, 2012)

Gazibo, M. (2020). Military. In Lynch, G., & VonDoepp, P. (Eds.). *Routledge handbook of democratization in Africa.* London: Routledge, 174–87.

Gbaguidi, A. (September 14, 2016). Bénin : le maire d'Abomey, Blaise Ahanhanzo Glèlè sous menace de destitution. *Benin Monde Info.* http://beninmonde infos.com/index.php/benin/19-politique/3447-benin-le-maire-d-abomey-blaise-ahanhanzo-glele-sous-menace-de-destitution (accessed December 30, 2016)

Government of Burkina Faso. (n.d.). *Litige frontalier Mali–Burkina Faso, Affrontement de noël 1985 une guerre absurd.* Centre National Archives du Burkina Faso.

Gyimah-Boadi, E. (Ed.). (2004). *Democratic reform in Africa — The quality of progress.* Boulder: Lynne Rienner.

———. (2009). Another step forward for Ghana. *Journal of Democracy, 20*(2), 138–52.

Harakova, H. (2011). Introduction: The Predicament of the Concept of Power in Africa. In Horakova, H., Nugent, P., & Skalnik, P. (Eds.). *Africa: Power and Powerlessness.* Munster: LIT Verlag, 9–21.

Hassani, K. (October 20, 2016). Bénin : pour un encadrement de la destitution des maires. *Contrepoints.* https://www.contrepoints.org/2016/10/20/269442-benin-encadrement-de-destitution-maires (accessed December 27, 2016)

Herbst, J. (2000). *States and power in Africa*. Princeton: Princeton University Press.

International Court of Justice. (1986a). *Communiqué: Chamber of Court to hear Burkina Faso and Mali on possible indication of provisional measures*. No. 86/1, January 6, 1986.

———. (1986b). *Communiqué: Provisional measures are indicated in the case of the Frontier Dispute (Burkina Faso–Mali)*. No. 86/2, January 10, 1986.

———. (1986c). *Communiqué: Frontier Dispute (Burkina Faso/Republic of Mali) judgment of the Chamber*. No. 86/18, December 22, 1986.

———. (1986d). *Reports of judgments, advisory opinions and orders, case concerning the Frontier Dispute* (Burkina Faso/Republic of Mali). Judgment of December 22, 1986.

———. (2013). *Frontier Dispute (Burkina Faso/Niger)*. Judgment of April 16, 2013.

Iwata, T. (2000). La conférence nationale souveraine et la démocratisation au Togo du point de vue de la société civile. *Africa Development, 25*(3–4), 135–60.

———. (2004). *Democratic transition and civil society in Africa*. Tokyo: Kokusai Shoin. (Published in Japanese)

———. (2011). Decentralization and Election in Benin. *Insight on Africa* (African Studies Association of India), *3*(2), 101–15.

———. (2012a). Political Sphere of Mayor in the Time of Decentralization. In Masahisa Kawabata, M., & Ochiai, T. (Eds.). *Africa and the World (Afurika to Sekai)*. Kyoto: Koyo Shobo, 144–64. (Published in Japanese)

———. (2012b). Comparative Study on "Asian" Approaches to Africa: An Introductory Reflection. *African Studies Monographs, 33*(4), 209–31.

———. (2016a). Border and Regional Security in Local Governments' Cooperation in West Africa: Case Studies in Burkina Faso. *Ritsumeikan Annual Review of International Relations, 15*, 1–25.

———. (2016b). Laughter in Political Transition in Africa. *Ritsumeikan Studies in Language and Culture, 2*(4), 133–55.

———. (2017). Rethinking the concept of power in African Politics — A boundary producer. *Ritsumeikan Annual Review of International Studies, 16*, 19–36.

———. (2018). Political impact of decentralization in Africa. *Ritsumeikan Annual Review of International Studies, 17*, 1–25.

———. (Ed.). (2020a). *New Asian Approaches to Africa — Rivalries and Collaborations*. Wilmington: Vernon Press.

———. (2020b). A Turning Point in Japan's Soft Power Strategy in Africa. In Iwata, T. (Ed.). *New Asian Approaches to Africa — Rivalries and Collaborations*. Wilmington: Vernon Press, 161–78.

———. (2020c). Political Satire and Laughter in Africa. In Ofusu-Kusi, Y., & Matsuda, M. (Eds.). *The Challenge of Africa Potentials — Conviviality, Informality and Futurity*. Bamenda: Langaa, 143–68.

———. (2021). Revisiting Border Issues in Africa: a reflection on the border of the French colony Upper Volta. *Ritsumeikan Annual Review of International Studies, 20*, 12–23.

———. (2022a). Rethinking Democratization in Contemporary African Politics. *Ritsumeikan Annual Review of International Studies, 21*, 1–27.

──────. (2022b). Las relaciones entre Asia y Africa en el pasado y el futuro. *Cuadernos de Nuestra America*, No.6, CIPI (Cuba), 160–71.

Jackson, R., & Rosberg, C. (1984). Personal Rule: Theory and Practice in Africa. *Comparative Politics, 16*(4), 421–42.

Jaffré, B. (1997). *Biographie de Thomas Sankara.* Paris: Harmattan.

Jan, P. (May 9, 2015). CIJ. Nouvelle frontière entre le Burkina Faso et le Niger. Effacement des dernières traces de la colonisation. *Droitpublic.net.* http://www.droitpublic.net/imprimersans.php3?id_article=5216&nom_site=Droit public.net&url_site=http://www.droitpublic.net (accessed June 21, 2015)

Japan External Trade Organization (JETRO) & Confederation of Indian Industry (CII). (2019). *Analysis Paper on Platform for Japan–India Business Cooperation in Asia–Africa Region.*

Jeune Afrique. (May 9, 2015, 2015a). Nouvelle frontière Burkina Faso–Niger: 18 communes changeront de pays. http://www.jeuneafrique.com/Article/DEPAFP20150509104940/diplomatie-diplomatie-nouvelle-fronti-re-burkina-faso-niger-18-communes-changeront-de-pays.html (accessed May 10, 2015)

──────. (October 9, 2015, 2015b). Burkina Faso: trois gendarmes tués lors d'une attaque près de la frontière malienne. http://www.jeuneafrique.com/270720/politique/burkina-faso-3-gendarmes-tues-lors-dune-attaque-pres-de-frontiere-malienne (accessed October 10, 2015)

──────. (December 25, 2015, 2015c). *Il y a trente ans éclatait la « guerre de Noël » entre le Mali et le Burkina Faso.* http://www.jeuneafrique.com/288381/politique/il-y-a-quarante-ans-eclatait-la-guerre-de-noel-entre-le-mali-et-le-burkina (accessed December 27, 2015)

──────. (January 17, 2016, 2016a). Le Burkina sous le choc après avoir été frappé par la terreur jihadiste. http://www.jeuneafrique.com/294466/politique/le-burkina-frappe-par-la-terreur-jihadiste (accessed January 17, 2016)

──────. (January 20, 2016, 2016b). Attentat de Ouagadougou: trois assaillants sont encore recherchés, selon Manuel Valls. http://www.jeuneafrique.com/295130/politique/attentat-de-ouagadougou-trois-assaillants-recherches-selon-manuel-valls (accessed January 27, 2016)

──────. (2016c). No. 2872, January 24–30.

Jockers, H., Dirk, K., & Nugent, P. (2010). The successful Ghana election of 2008: A convenient myth? *Journal of Modern African Studies, 48*(1), 95–115.

Journal du Jeudi. (February 4–10, 2010). No. 959.

──────. (June 2–8, 2016). No. 1289.

Kaplan, R-D. (2012). *The Revenge of Geography.* New York: Random House.

Kim, H-S. (2020). Korea–Africa Forum (KOAF) — South Korea's Middle Power Diplomacy and Its Limitations. In Iwata, T. (Ed.). *New Asian Approaches to Africa — Rivalries and Collaborations.* Wilmington: Vernon Press, 53–82.

Kindo, B. (June 1, 2016). Attaques de Ouagadougou: 6 individus arrêtés. http://www.omegabf.net/societe/attaques-de-ouagadougou-6-individus-arretes (accessed June 1, 2016)

King, K., & Venkatachalam, M. (2021). Reflections on India–Africa Studies, Development Cooperation, and Soft Power. In King, K., & Venkatachalam, M. (Eds.). (2021). *India's Development Diplomacy and Soft Power in Africa.* Woodbridge–New York: James Currey, 185–96.

Kragelund, P. (2019). *South–South Development.* New York: Routledge.

Kurtz, D. (2001). *Political Anthropology — Paradigm and Power.* Boulder: Westview.

Lamizana, S. (1999). *Mémoires: Sous les drapeaux* (Vol. 2). Paris: Jaguar Conseil.

Levitsky, S., & Way, L. A. (2010). *Competitive authoritarianism: Hybrid regimes after the Cold War.* Cambridge: Cambridge University Press.

Lindberg, S. (Ed.). (2009). *Democratization by elections — A new model of transition.* Baltimore: Johns Hopkins University Press.

———. (2010). What accountability pressures do MPs in Africa face and how do they respond? Evidence from Ghana. *Journal of Modern African Studies, 48*(1), 117–42.

Lukes, S. (1986). *Power.* New York: New York University Press.

Mamdani, M. (1996). *Citizen and Subject: Contemporary Africa and the Legacy of Late Colonialism.* Princeton: Princeton University Press.

Mawdsley, E. (2012). *From Recipients to Donors — Emerging powers and the changing development landscape.* London: Zed Books.

Médard, J-F. (1990). L'État patrimonialisé. *Politique Africaine, 39,* 25–36.

Melly, P. (2023). Niger coup underlines challenge to democracy across West Africa. Chatham House. https://www.chathamhouse.org/2023/08/niger-coup-underlines-challenge-democracy-across-west-africa (accessed August 31, 2023)

Métodjo, A-K. (2008). *Devenir Maire en Afrique.* Paris: Harmattan.

Meton, A. (February 14, 2017). Destitution des maires au Bénin : Ouidah, une ville plus que spécifique. *Informateur.* http://www.linformateurbenin.info/destitution-des-maires-au-benin-ouidah-une-ville-plus-que-specifique (accessed February 26, 2017)

(Le) Monde Afrique. (May 9, 2015). Nouvelle frontière entre le Burkina Faso et le Niger, 18 communes vont changer de pays. http://www.lemonde.fr/afrique/article/2015/05/09/nouvelle-frontiere-entre-le-burkina-faso-et-le-niger-18-communes-vont-changer-de-pays_4630513_3212.html#hA1bEp75 bKjh8mkT.99 (accessed June 21, 2015)

Morreall, J. (Ed.). (1987). *The Philosophy of Laughter and Humor.* Albany: State University of New York Press.

Mthembu, P. (2018). *China and India's Development Cooperation in Africa — The Rise of Southern Powers.* Cham: Palgrave MacMillan.

Mukherjee, R. (2021). India and Japan's Grand Bargain in the Context of China's Rise. In Bekkevold. J. I., & Kalyanaraman. S. (Eds.). *India's Great Power Politics: Managing China's Rise.* London: Routledge, 247–61.

Nabole, I-I. (December 7, 2016). Arrondissement n°8 de Ouaga : Après la destitution du maire, les machettes ont parlé. *Burkina24.* http://burkina24.com/2016/12/07/arrondissement-n8-de-ouaga-apres-la-destitution-du-maire-les-machettes-ont-parle (accessed March 6, 2017)

———. (December 10, 2016). Arrondissement n°8 : Ce qui est reproché à l'ancien maire Mahamadi Zongo. *Burkina24.* https://burkina24.com/2016/12/10/arrondissement-n8-ce-qui-est-reproche-a-lancien-maire-mahamadi-zongo (accessed March 6, 2017)

———. (May 29, 2017). Municipales 2017 : Les résultats provisoires des 19 communes. *Burkina24*. https://burkina24.com/2017/05/29/municipales-2017-les-resultats-provisoires-des-19-communes (accessed June 7, 2017)

Nassa, D. (2008). Dynamisme d'une ville stimulé par la frontière: l'example de Ouangolodougou au Nord de la Côte d'Ivoire. *HAL*. https://halshs.archives-ouvertes.fr/halshs-00261598 (accessed December 22, 2014)

Nations Online Project. Political Map of Africa. https://www.nationsonline. org/oneworld/map/africa-political-map.htm (accessed April 12, 2024)

Nugent, P. (2002). *Smugglers, secessionists & loyal citizens on the Ghana–Togo Frontier*. Oxford: James Currey.

Nye, J. (2004). *Soft Power — The Means to Success in World Politics*. New York: Public Affairs.

OECD Sahel and West Africa Club (OECD–SWAC). (2010). Mali – Burkina Faso, Cross-border Co-operation: Operational Framework Proposals and Policy Recommendations. http://www.oecd.org/countries/burkinafaso/47028005.pdf (accessed January 13, 2015)

OECD. (October 25, 2021). From emerging donor to global development partner. https://www.oecd.org/country/korea/thematic-focus/from-emerging -donor-to-global-development-partner-66044045 (accessed July 19, 2022)

Opalo, K. O. (2012). African elections: Two divergent trends. *Journal of Democracy, 23*(3), 80–93.

Ottaway, M. (Ed.). (2003). *Democracy challenged: The rise of semi-authoritarianism*. Washington D.C.: Carnegie Endowment for International Peace.

Owa, M. (2020). Changing Aid Architecture in Africa through the Encounter between OECD Countries and non-OECD Countries. In Iwata, T. (Ed.). *New Asian Approaches to Africa — Rivalries and Collaborations*. Wilmington: Vernon Press, 237–62.

Pan, H. (2020). A New Approach to Cooperation with Africa from the Rise of Chinese Outbound Tourism in the 21st Century. In Iwata, T. (Ed.). *New Asian Approaches to Africa — Rivalries and Collaborations*. Wilmington: Vernon Press, 135–60.

Panapress. (May 13, 2003). Ivorian Civil War Cuts Abidjan Port Activities by 43.4 Percent. http://www.panapress.com/ivorian-civil-war-cuts-Abidjan-port-activities-by-43.4-percent--13-482303-18-lang1-index.html (accessed April 18, 2016)

Panda, J-P. (Ed.). (2020). *Scaling India–Japan Cooperation in Indo-Pacific and Beyond 2025 — Corridor, Connectivity and Contours*. New Delhi: KW Publisher.

Partenariat pour le Développement Municipal (PDM). (2006). *Annuaire de la zone transfrontalière; Sikasso–Korhogo–Bobo Dioulasso*.

(Le) Pays (Burkinabe newspaper). February 12, 2010.

———. Website. March 18, 2018.

Piqué, F., & Rainer, L-H. (1999). *Les Bas-reliefs d'Abomey: l'Histoire racontée sur les murs*. Cotonou: Les Editions du Flamboyant.

Purushothaman, C. (2021). *Emerging Powers, Development Cooperation and South–South Relations*. Cham: Palgrave Macmillan.

Radio France Internationale (RFI). (March 14, 2016). Côte d'Ivoire: une attaque revendiquée par Aqmi frappe Grand-Bassam. http://www.rfi.fr/afrique/20160313-cote-ivoire-tirs-entendus-grand-bassam (accessed March 14, 2016)

Raposo de Medeiros Carvalho, P.M. (2020). Small Farmers — The Missing Link in the ProSavana Triangle. In Iwata, T. (Ed.). *New Asian Approaches to Africa — Rivalries and Collaborations*. Wilmington: Vernon Press, 181–210.

Republic of Mozambique, Ministry of Agriculture and Food Security (MASA). (2015). *Report of the public hearing outcome of the ProSAVANA's Draft Zero Master Plan.*

République du Mali. (1985). *Memoire: Affaire du differend frontalier Burkina Faso/Mali* (Vol. 2).

Research and Information System for Developing Countries. About AAGC. https://aagc.ris.org.in/en/about-aagc (accessed July 29, 2023)

Research and Information System for Developing Countries, Economic Research Institute for ASEAN and East Asia, & Institute of Developing Economies – Japan External Trade Organization (2017). *A Vision Document: Asia Africa Growth Corridor.*

Saito, F. (Ed.). (2008). *Foundations for Local Governance — Decentralization in Comparative Perspective.* Heidelberg: Physica-Verlag.

Sarkar M. G., & Panda, J. (2021). Between Business and Balance: India–Japan in Africa vis-à-vis China. In King. K., & Venkatachalam, M. (Eds.). *India's Development Diplomacy and Soft Power in Africa.* Woodbridge–New York: James Currey, 41–56.

Schaeffer, J-M. (2011). Rire et blaguer. In Birnbaum, J. (Ed.). *Pourquoi rire?* Paris: Gallimard, 23–37.

Schedler, A. (Ed) (2006). *Electoral Authoritarianism.* Boulder: Lynne Rienner.

Schmitter, P. C., & Karl, T. L. (2009). What democracy is… and is not. In Diamond, L. (Ed.). *Democracy a reader.* Baltimore: Johns Hopkins University Press, 3–16.

Seiyama, K. (2000). *Power.* Tokyo: Univerisity of Tokyo Press. (Published in Japanese)

Skinner, E. (1964). *The Mossi of the Upper Volta — The political development of the Sudanese people.* Stanford: Stanford University Press.

Slm, G. (September 7, 2016). Bénin : Patrice Talon fait destituer des Maires de l'Opposition. *Afrique sur 7.* http://www.afrique-sur7.fr/29405/benin-patrice-talon-fait-destituer-des-maires-de-lopposition (accessed December 27, 2016)

Sugita, A. (2000). *Power.* Tokyo: Iwanami. (Published in Japanese)

Takahashi, M. (2020). TICADs under the Changing Global Landscape — Japan's Role in African Development Reconsidered. In Iwata, T. (Ed.). *New Asian Approaches to Africa — Rivalries and Collaborations.* Wilmington: Vernon Press, 83–107.

Times of India. (July 25, 2022). India's push to boost Africa ties: 222 LoCs worth $14 billion. https://timesofindia.indiatimes.com/india/indias-push-to-boost-africa-ties-222-locs-worth-14-billion/articleshow/93097626.cms (accessed July 30, 2023)

Toulabor, C. (1986). *Le Togo sous Eyadéma.* Paris: Karthala.

———. (1991). La dérision politique en liberté à Lomé. *Politique Africaine, 43*, 136–41.

———. (1992a). Jeu de mots, jeu de vilains. Lexique de la derision politique au Togo. In Bayart, J-F. et al. (Eds.). *Le politique par le bas en Afrique Noire*. Paris: Karthala, 109–30.

———. (1992b) L'énonciation du pouvoir et de la richesse chez les jeunes ⟨ conjoncturés⟩ de Lomé, In Bayart, J-F. et al. (Eds.). *Le politique par le bas en Afrique Noire*. Paris: Karthala, 131–45.

———. (1993). Le culte Eyadéma au Togo, In Bayart, J-F. (Ed.). *Religion et modernité politique en Afrique noire*. Paris: Karthala, 277–97.

———. (1996). Les mots sont fatigués ou la désillusion démocratique au Togo? *Politique Africaine, 64*, 62–72.

Touval, S. (1972). *The boundary politics of independent Africa*. Cambridge: Harvard University Press.

UNCDF. (2012). *LOBI/UEMOA, Initiatives transfrontalières de développement local pour l'Afrique de l'Ouest.*

US Department of State. (2021). *Summit for democracy*. https://www.state.gov/summit-for-democracy/ (accessed December 10, 2021)

Van de Walle, N. (2003). Presidentialism and clientelism in Africa's emerging party systems. *Journal of Modern African Studies, 41*(2), 297–321.

Venkatachalam, M., & King, K. (2021). India–Africa Now: Changing Imaginaries and Knowledge Paradigms. In King, K., & Venkatachalam, M. (Eds.). (2021). *India's Development Diplomacy and Soft Power in Africa*. Woodbridge–New York: James Currey, 1–23.

Verschave, F-X. (2000). *La Françafrique: le plus long scandale de la République*. Paris: Stock.

Weber, M. (1971). *Economie et société*. Paris: Plon.

West African Borders and Integration. (2004). *Cross-Border Diaries*, No.00.

———. (2005). (Workshop Report) *Deuxième atelier du réseau frontières et intégrations en Afrique de l'ouest*. Abuja, October 27–29, 2004.

———. (2006). *Cross-Border Diaries*, No.04.

———. (2007a). *Cross-Border Diaries*, No.06.

———. (2007b). *Cross-Border Diaries*, No.07.

White House (June 26, 2022). FACT SHEET: President Biden and G7 Leaders Formally Launch the Partnership for Global Infrastructure and Investment. https://www.whitehouse.gov/briefing-room/statements-releases/2022/06/26/fact-sheet-president-biden-and-g7-leaders-formally-launch-the-partnership-for-global-infrastructure-and-investment/ (accessed June 27, 2022)

World Bank. Data: GDP (current USD, 1990). https://data.worldbank.org/indicator/Ny.Gdp.Mktp.Cd?end=1990&most_recent_value_desc=true&start=1960 (accessed July 8, 2022)

World Bank. Data: GDP (current USD, 2021). https://data.worldbank.org/indicator/Ny.Gdp.Mktp.Cd?end=2021&most_recent_value_desc=true&start=1960 (accessed July 8, 2022)

Wu, Y.-S. (2020). The Forum on China–Africa Cooperation (FOCAC) — a Co-constituted Relationship. In Iwata, T. (Ed.). (2020). *New Asian Approaches to Africa — Rivalries and Collaborations*. Wilmington: Vernon Press, 3–30.

Yatta, P.-F. (2011). *Analyse du couloir économique Sikasso–Orodara*. Fédération Canadienne des Municipalités.

Zoure, A. (November 18, 2014). Burkina: Les Conseils municipaux et régionaux sont dissous. *Burkina 24*. http://www.burkina24.com/2014/11/18/burkina-les-conseils-municipaux-et-regionaux-sont-dissous (accessed November 19, 2014)

[Archives]

Archives nationales d'outre-mer [National Archives of Overseas]. Aix-en-Provence, France

Centre national des archives du Burkina Faso [National Center of Archives of Burkina Faso]. Ouagadougou, Burkina Faso

Archives nationales du Sénégal [National Archives of Senegal]. Dakar, Senegal

Index

www.ingramcontent.com/pod-product-compliance
Lightning Source LLC
Chambersburg PA
CBHW050515280326
41932CB00014B/2332